A DAD FOR ALL SEASONS

How My Sons Raised Me

IAN MUCKLEJOHN

GIBSON SQUARE

*For Piers, Ian and Lars without whom none
of this would have been possible and for whom this book
has been written with the hope that others may enjoy it, too.
Here are the 'pictures in words' of your early childhood.*

A DAD FOR ALL SEASONS

First edition published in the UK by Gibson Square

info@gibsonsquare.com
www.gibsonsquare.com
Tel: +44 (0)20 7096 1100 (UK)
Tel: +1 646 216 9813 (USA)
Tel: +353 (0)1 657 1057 (Eire)

ISBN   9781906142711

Contents

Foreword

If risk-taking were an Olympic sport, Ian Mucklejohn would be the gold medal winner. Imagine, as a single man, and an orphan, and a single child yourself, deciding to create a family. What a risk he took, a man alone. What an adventure it has been. And what a triumphant success he has made of it.

He not only found two surrogate mothers to supply the eggs and the womb but also had the most amazing luck, the eggs took, and Ian fathered three lovely babies. That was eleven years ago, and as it turns out, that was the easy bit. As this book reveals, life has not been easy for them all. But the good news is that the risk was well worth taking. Those babies are now funny, clever, beautifully-brought-up triplet boys.

I can't imagine how he has achieved all this because I know from my own experience what it's like to have to have three children. God gave you two hands, two arms, two ears and two eyes. Holding on to three, keeping three in your sight and your hearing, carrying three at a time normally requires help. It's not just a physical challenge, but an emotional one as well. With three, there is always a middle child, who howls with rage if he or she suspects the oldest or the youngest has an unfair advantage. In my case I had a husband to rely on, a sister to telephone for help, and my parents as grandparents to act as spare hands, arms, eyes and ears, and adjudicators when the inevitable rows broke out. Ian does it all by himself, and as this book reveals, juggles, organizes, cooks, keeps sane, stays calm, and handles every obstacle in his path triumphantly.

This is not a how-to book, but I imagine many parents, and, above all, many fathers, will find it funny, moving, and really helpful. In these pages you will discover how to negotiate with an intransigent teacher who doesn't believe in competitive sports, how to deal with difficult questions about sex and death, and the best way to deal with so many other family dilemmas.

Knowing the Mucklejohns well, I have followed Ian's battles with political correctness, snobbery, prejudice, and in the end, cancer. And so far every battle has ended happily. As you read each chapter you will find that the boys, Ian, Piers and Lars, spring into vivid life. You will hugely enjoy their conversations as recorded lovingly in this book. And I have no doubt that you will end up being as awestruck by their father's achievement as I am. The boys are lucky to have him. He is immensely lucky to have them.

Esther Rantzen

Introduction

Parenting and plumbing have much in common. It's like stopping a leak in the dark with a duff torch while wearing mittens. You feel around, try to understand what's happening, make a decision, and then after the event spend forever justifying it in the voice of sweet reason tricked out with a spoonful of authority. The trouble is that the world moves on with such speed that the lessons learned from one's own childhood seem as well matched as a quill pen scratching on the surface of an iPad.

I've been a dad for 12 years. That in itself isn't unusual. But what is somewhat rarer is that I have triplet sons and that I am a single dad. It was a Big Thing at the time but that feels a lifetime ago now. As a parent you are thrown in at the deep end from the very beginning. What came before your children doesn't really matter any longer. You can't imagine what your life used to be like. In my case, I was outnumbered from day one...

This book started life as a diary I kept off and on over the years. It is patched together out of the treasure trove of memories that accumulated watching my three babies grow into three boys. In addition to the photographs, I hope these stories will amuse (and not embarrass too much) my sons and their loved ones when they are grown-ups.

More than a decade on, I picked the best ones and thought

others might enjoy sharing in the joys and frustrations of parenthood. The stories are organised by the things we deal with as parents – the awkward questions, the fights and crocodile tears, the hilarious moments, the tough ones that make you question your judgment. My children's experiences are all here and maybe your family's as well – just multiply by three and deduct one parent.

1

A Dad for All Seasons

'Oh, come off it, boys. It's only seven o'clock.'

'Yes, Dad, and we're already dressed and our teeth brushed. We went down at six to see if Santa has been. And he has. Come on. It's time to go down. We want a short breakfast. Just some cold Cocopops. Served quickly. Please.'

A few minutes later, wrapping paper was being shredded. The choices on their Christmas lists had been eclectic. 'Ian's head and Lars's head' were on Piers' list. 'A baby boy' had been on Ian's. 'I'll bring him up so he'll be better than my brothers,' Ian had assured me.

'Do my sweet grabber first. It just needs a few batteries. Oh and the grabbing thing's twisted. And the sweets are coming out. It's all your fault, Dad. You just don't bother.'

'I'm just sorting out the money robot. I need a Philips screwdriver that's just a tiny bit smaller than the one I have.'

'And what about my ATM bank?'

'Just working out the date and time which I need to put in before your PIN.'

'I'm putting all my money in.'

'You need to put more money in,' said the robot. 'You've nearly reached your target.'

'My limit, more likely,' I muttered as the third money

machine was presented for battery fixing.

'Have a nice day,' said the machine.

'Da-ad, what about my flipping rat?'

'Just going to make it flip. Let it charge-up first.'

'But it's had ages to do that. Can you do my helicopter instead?'

'That's got to charge-up, too.'

'What's £29.50 short of £50?'

'Hang on. That's too complicated for seven thirty on Christmas morning. Let me just get these batteries into the turkey. No, I mean the banking robot.'

'But that's why I need to know. My target is £50 and I've only got £29.50.'

'Can we play Lars-opoly?'

'When I've got the batteries in and the turkey basted. Oh – and who sent you these gifts you've just opened? Best not open all these kits at the same time or we'll get in a muddle.'

'But they're our toys, Dad.'

'When can we use the Wii?'

'When I've got the batteries out of the turkey and into the robots and the butter off my fingers and onto the turkey.'

'Why aren't you dressed yet, Dad? Someone might come.'

'And don't tell me I might embarrass you in my dressing gown.'

'My Wii control won't work. Only Lars's will.'

'I'll look in the instructions in a mo. Just use Lars's for now.'

'But we don't want to share. They're our presents.'

'Put some in. You've nearly reached your limit,' said the movement-activated robot.

'OK. Let's read the instruction book. I'll just get it out of the bin.'

'I was only tidying up.'

'Thanks, Ian. Kind thought, but sometimes a bit quick.'

'I want my control to be first. Why won't it work?'

'Because I have to crawl on the floor to the main controller which, thankfully, I had someone install for me well before Christmas, and get it to shake hands with the controller.'

'Why do you want it to do that?'

'So it can develop a lasting relationship with it.'

'Why have you trodden on my sweet, Dad?'

'Just for fun, Piers.'

'Can we play Lars-opoly now? You said.'

'We'll have lunch first.'

'But why have you overcooked the brussels?'

'These are chestnuts, darling. They're yummy.'

'I hate them.'

'You've never had them before, Piers.'

'That's why I hate them.'

'I hate parsnips.'

'I've done them in honey.'

'Hate honey.'

'This is yummy,' said Lars. 'It doesn't taste of anything.'

'Have a nice day,' said the robot.

'Do you need the loo, Piers?'

'No. Why?'

'You're hopping from foot to foot and clutching yourself.'

'Then I'll walk in slow motion. Like this.'

'Shut the door, Lars, you'll let the heat out.'

'You don't let the heat out, Daddy, you let the cold in. Mr P. said this. He's the Head of Science. And he's 35 and he's been at our school for seven years.'

'Thanks, Lars, I'll bear this in mind. Just shut the door anyway, please.'

Enough to make me take to the cooking sherry, if we had any, I thought. Was Christmas like this for my parents? Was I so perpetually demanding, so opinionated, so essentially ungrateful? Was life a tennis match of similarly gently barbed comments? Or was this all what I had quite intentionally brought on myself? Meaning of life – or Christmas dinner? I comforted myself by peeling the brussels sprouts – the one and only part of the traditional meal that they liked.

2

Beginnings

Cold sore cream and dustard dreams

'That would be assault.'

I dropped little Lars's hand.

'But he's not yet five. He can't put it on himself.'

I pocketed the tube of Boots Cold Sore Cream. His teacher smiled at me. She was sweet and all three boys spoke of her warmly the previous day – their first day at school. Her name had been the first to be mentioned when the list of those they should invite to their fifth birthday party had been discussed round the breakfast table. I had asked if she could put a dab of cream on Lars's cold sore in the middle of the day. It was not yet visible, but he had the forewarning tingling sensation well-known to sufferers that one is on the way.

'If we apply something like that, it would be assault. He has to apply it himself. Yes, it's silly, but that's the way it is.'

'OK. I'll come in at lunchtime. Oh, and he's having a touch of melancholia because Piers is going to the doctor and he wonders if he'll come back. I've told him he will, but once he gets something into his head. Well, you know.' My voice trailed away.

'What I'm saying is that he'd love a cuddle. Are you still able to cuddle?' Seeing the nodded assent, I added 'Well, we'll take advantage of that while it's still allowed. Oh, and we're coming up for a birthday party. I think there are some new friends they'd like to invite. Do you think you could have a chat with them while the boys and girls are around them and let me have a list? I can print out some more invites.'

It seemed like a logical request, albeit demanding of a minute or two's time, so the momentary flicker of panic came as a surprise. My mind raced. How had I transgressed this time?

'We can write down the first names, but not the surnames – of course.'

I paused, awaiting some elucidation. Perhaps the word 'security' might be murmured, or even 'confidentiality'. The sentence ended with 'of course', so I should know the reason instinctively. My boys might find out their classmates' surnames and tell me. Unless they wore paper bags over their heads, they might recognise each other in the street. What on earth was the risk in letting me have surnames to distinguish one Emily from another? Maybe I should be getting used to this new society in which we are ruled by fear – sometimes of litigation, but generally simply fear itself. What a far cry from my own infant school days in the '50s when parents' names and addresses would have been scribbled down for me. What have we gained compared to the trust we have lost? I looked forward to the 'Friends' meeting that the boys had brought home a letter about. 'Go direct to the kitchen door', the instructions had read. I found a room with a kettle. Must be it.

A group of women who clearly knew each other well were discussing events for the infants. A circus. Great! A travelling theatre company. Splendid!

'Now who can go to court to get the licence? It has to be someone who can be there on the day.'

'Why do you need a licence for these performances?'

'So that we can serve alcohol.'

'But isn't that a bit incongruous?' I hesitated, aware that I was on new and untried ground. 'I mean infants and booze. I'm probably coming from another direction, but I can't reconcile the two. I give assurances to parents of my students that there won't be any alcohol on the premises. I've just come back from Norway and certainly the Scandinavians would think I'd gone bonkers if I brought liquor into my school.'

'Part of our culture. Wouldn't get the dads in if we didn't have refreshments.'

'But need they be intoxicating?'

The Headmistress smiled at me, keen to move on.

'We don't expect our children to drink,' she confided, reassur ingly.

I had expected that I would learn a few lessons at infant school. These were too many, too soon. No doubt, I would adjust. It was just that I felt I didn't want to. Assault by cold sore cream, the secrecy of surnames, tots with tots — an unlikely juxtapositioning of homonyms. It was life on Mars.

Getting them to their infant school was multitasking writ large.

'I don't like being me.'

Ian was sitting Buddha-style, staring into the mirror, closing first one eye, then the other as he squinted into the mirror. I had heard it once before, instantly alerted his teacher and been assured that a programme of positive affirmation of self-image would be instituted at once. The blitz on self-confidence had clearly been resisted, so I sat down in front of him. 'Don't compare' was what I had been told from the outset. I thought I would give it a try this time, though.

'But you can do lots of things very well, Ian. You can blow your nose better than Lars. You can wipe your bottom better than Piers. You can twirl spaghetti round your fork better than both of them.'

Yet, he was still asking for 'Dustard Dream' biscuits with his bedtime milk, rarely benefited from the morning chocolate bribe for nocturnal continence and was generally moved into the corridor to change into pyjamas for clouting his brothers with toys they were playing with that he, therefore, wanted. My face had crumpled into genuine concern.

'So what's really the problem, darling? You know you're a super boy and Daddy loves you. You're you and you're very special for Daddy.'

He sighed and looked glumly at his reflection in that small part of the floor-to-ceiling mirror on the wardrobe door that was not covered with scribbles of dragons, dinosaurs and hand-prints. His troubled blue eyes met mine. 'It's orange.' He pulled at his hair. 'Lars's is red. I want mine to be red, not orange.'

Relieved that it was not a personality transplant that was required, I proceeded to deal with the getting-ready-for-school scenario that would be my lot for the next 13 years.

The everything allergy

'What's for breakfast?' Lars was polishing the basin in the bath-room. Today was one of the days he would do 'all the work'. Some days he would only do some because he had 'too much to do'.

'Maybe toast,' I said, absent-mindedly. 'No, you won't be downstairs in time. It could be cereal this morning.'

'I'm allergic to toast,' he mentioned as he passed from nursery to en-suite.

'Now where did you get this from? I've told you that this family doesn't get ill. We eat sensibly, use our feet and keep healthy. You've seen all your friends take time off school and most of the staff at nursery have been away sometime or other. But not you and your brothers. And when was the last time

Daddy was ill? Never. You're very healthy.' Realising I had wandered off at a tangent, I readdressed the question. 'Who's been talking to you about allergies? We don't have them. They're for other people.'

'And I'm allergic to cereal – and milk,' he added. 'And everything.'

'Well you're not. I'll have to have a word with your teacher about these ideas. I'll hear no more about it. Now look, you've cleaned the basin before doing your teeth. Get your toothbrush out and kill all the bacteria. They're laughing at you. Ha Ha, they're saying, we can play on your teeth. We can just slide up and down them. I think I can hear them now. That's the way. I can hear them yelling now. Brush with vigour and they'll all be dead.'

It seemed to work. Drying between the toes was designed to prevent the bacteria eating the skin there. Shampooing the hair in the shower was a 'cootie egg-hunt'. The more graphic the need for the ablution, the more energetic the application.

In time, I found I could get all three from sleeping, through showering, toothbrushing, dressing, room tidying, all breakfasted and walked to school in an hour and a quarter.

School run

This particular day had started early. A distant voice was chanting, 'It's too dark. It's too dark.'

I opened the bedroom door. A small figure in blue-striped pyjamas, Pilchard the cat tucked under one arm, head bowed in the knowledge that a wrong was being done, shifted from foot to foot. 'It's too-ooo dark, Daddy.'

'What do you expect at half past three in the morning? Come on, little one, give me your hand. It's bitterly cold.'

'But why do you turn the light out before it's good morning

time? It makes it too dark and I can't see.'

Toying briefly with the idea of a discussion about the merits of energy saving by turning lights off, I decided to retain the vestiges of sleep still clinging to me and walked Ian back to his bed with half-closed eyes.

'Here you are darling and here you stay.'

'But, Daddy, it's still too dark.'

'And it'll remain so. If you have a dry night, there'll be a chocolate for you in the morning. If you wake Daddy again, there won't. OK?'

'OK, Daddy.'

The following morning three white shirts and three blue tops with gold insignia were pulled over tousled heads. Three pairs of grey trousers were pulled over bottoms. Having extricated and rotated one back-to-front white shirt from under a blue top and sorted out a back-to-front pair of grey trousers, we were ready to leave.

'Now you've finished your cornflakes, put your long-sleeved top on, Ian.'

En route to the top of the head, the clean and folded garment removed the customary milk moustache.

'But I want to hold your hand properly.'

The hand was already grasped by another. I offered a thumb.

'Naaaah. I don't want that. I want your hand.'

'Look, I haven't got another full hand.' My mind flailed. 'Take Daddy's leg.'

A grotesque three-legged race of four people lurched down the road as the time ticked by to the start of the school day.

'My hands are cold. I want my gloves on. No, not like that, I've got too many fingers.'

'I've got bogies. I want a tissue.'

Now gloved, nose-wiped and with legs freed by the promise of a hand after crossing the road, we moved purposefully towards the heart-stopping part of our morning walk – the main road. The previous day, Lars and Piers holding my hands and Ian holding Piers', we had crossed at my command. A change of mind on Ian's part and he had slipped his hand from Piers' grasp. I had taken two over. One remained, tiny and frightened, on the other side with streams of rush-hour traffic between us. Leaving two tiny figures on the other side, I dashed back, raised a hand and marched a reluctant Ian back to his brothers. A child in each hand and a thumb on the hood of the third one's coat, I spotted a gap and yelled 'Cross!'

'Waaah. You're holding my coat.' Stopping briefly at a familiar part of the worn white line with a car bearing down on each side, I used the fabric as a lever to propel the reluctant walker out of imminent danger. It took the distance of the remaining carriageway for the zip to come completely open by which time the expected 'You pulled my coat open' could receive the customary response 'Well, do it up again.'

The muddy track that connected the main road with the housing estate in which their school lay ended in a short span of newly-laid gravel, presumably part of the deal to give a new house planning permission.

'Bob the Builder's been here, Daddy.' The nascent garden resembled a tip. 'And left some litter behind.'

'Just as long as you don't, darlings.'

We had three road junctions to negotiate in the remaining five minutes before the school doors were closed. Avoiding the small pile of vomit that we had noticed for the last several days without rain, we passed a new iced-bun wrapper next to a soft drink can we already knew from their first day and a red post office rubber band that had recently come to adorn a patch of what could have been mud, but may have been something altogether more sinister.

'Looks like poo, Daddy.'

'If it looks like poo, it may well be poo, boys. We won't probe it. Oh, and here's another pile of cat vomit.'

'Did it have eyes? The cat.' Ian added as an afterthought. Then, remembering that the presence or absence of eyes were attributes generally in his questions about insects – questions to which he never wanted answers – he grabbed for another query. 'Was it black?'

'Almost certainly, Ian. Now hold Daddy's hand.'

'Where's the first cat sick? I wanna see the first cat sick. Waaaah.' For half a minute, Lars remained motionless, demanding sight of the small beige pile that had been passed, unremarked, some minutes before. I put him under my arm.

'Next?'

Their school was in sight. There it was, just on the other side of a main road with two other roads leading into it, the continuation of the pavement on the other side blocked by parked cars between the chicanes of which through traffic on the main road threaded.

'As soon as Daddy says 'cross!' you cross,' I yelled above the throb of a passing bus. A car driven by a parent emerging from one of the side roads kindly beckoned us to go over.

'Cross! Now.' I bellowed as Ian held back. He managed to pick up an interesting dead leaf before the jerk of his brother's arm almost knocked him off his feet. Past the house with eight cats, the boys looking low to see if they could see one skulking; past the house with an almost complete black and lichen 1952 Morris Oxford on the grass in front of it (was it a conceit or did I remember that very car parked in the same spot when I was a boy?); along to the school entrance; through the wooden gate, past the mud that might have been grass once and on to the open door of the boys' classroom, one of the three ladies who taught them standing with a welcoming smile. Our 15 minute walk had taken 20 this time and I knew that they were among the longest in my life.

Mind yer backs!

On my way back home, one of the boys' classmates' parents stopped to chat to me about the party. As we talked, an articulated lorry was backing into the school drive, hampered by residents' cars parked at the entrance. Inches from a lamp post on one side and a brick gatepost on the other, the rear swayed and shook as it ground to and fro, its exhaust gases steaming blue in the freezing air. Both of us made unspoken calculations of the distance we should be from each when it was felled and moved back. The Headmistress ran out, told the driver there was a tradesman's entrance and met us on her return. Within minutes we had agreed on an approach to the local council about pedestrian safety. I thought I was going to enjoy this one.

It was not to last.

Wouden it be nice…

'Can you come in, please?' The voice at the other end of the phone meant business. What had the boys been up to? 'With a pair of tweezers.'

'Tweezers?'

'Yes. Your own tweezers. Piers has a splinter in his finger.'

'You want me to get it out?'

'Yes, please.'

'Is he upset?'

'No.'

Within a few minutes, I was at the boys' state infant school. Piers, thumb extended, was waiting for me with a teacher.

'I've got a splinter, Daddy.'

'I can see that.' I wouldn't need the tweezers. A small piece of plant was sticking up above the skin. 'It's quite easy to pull out. Here you are. One small splinter removed.'

I turned to the teacher at his side. 'Forgive me for stating the obvious, but couldn't this be considered First Aid? When I was at school, you used to go to the Head's office and see the secretary who kept all manner of medical odds and ends by the typewriter…'

'It's a surgically invasive procedure.'

'A surgically invasive procedure.' I enunciated each word carefully, analysing the import of each, trying and failing to connect them with the insignificance of the small fleck of vegetation I had picked from the skin. I had just performed surgery without realising it.

'And if I'd been in London?'

'We'd have phoned the contact person you gave us.'

Little boy lost

The life of an only child and his parents is very different from the constant cut and thrust of the interrelationships between siblings. Clearly it was all coming my way from three directions because there was no other way for it to go. That was the way I had made it and it was up to me to make it work. Every day was a growing-up experience for all of us and every day I could see, with the help of my sons' perspective, the ludicrousness of everyday life. On the one hand, while the society of the second decade of the 21st century was tolerant of what would have been unthinkable in the rigid social context of the immediate post-war Britain into which I was born and out of which I was cast, on the other hand, in that time my sons could have played in the road.

'We've had reports of a lost child wandering alone, Sir. We're told he's five years old.'

'That's probably one of my sons. Actually, he's 10. He wanted to go for a walk on his own. Might it be him? Lars, will you get Ian and ask him if he went out of the gate?

On that Sunday afternoon, Ian had, indeed, taken a walk along the quiet cul-de-sac that we live in. It was the first time he had not been with his brothers. This simple and utterly normal event, this little bit of independence, had resulted in a police call out. An outside body had to be called in. And what was this telling me about societal attitudes? While I was musing about the sociological aspect, Ian burst into tears.

'I'm never going out again, Daddy!'

The journey to this point had not been without its other mini dramas.

The hug bug

'It's wrong.'

'No, it's not. It's good to have a hug.'

'Not at school. We're not to.'

'Martin came all the way from London to see you and just asked for a hug. You moved away. He was really quite surprised.'

'We're not allowed to touch at school.'

'Is there a reason?' I asked the Head.

'To prevent the spread of infection – and there might be an abused child in the class.'

'And there might not be. But children are very tactile. It goes against nature to stop them touching. And as for the abused child, well here's a chance to have good touching. There's every difference between this sort of touching and abusive touching.'

I bit my tongue. The words 'And if you can't tell the difference between the two, you shouldn't be able to make these damaging decisions' remained in my head. Sinister motivations were being attached to perfectly natural actions. Small children were being seen as causes of fear. What must it do to children to see that adults are afraid of them? I had a taste of this at the boys' swimming lessons.

'Never let them in the water. Just the slightest hint of an allegation from a parent and I'd be finished.'

The swimming school's owner was friendly enough, but he was adamant. The few male instructors stood, dressed, at the side of the pool, giving instructions from there. Only the female teachers were in the water with the children.

'Come off it, Larry. That's quite an insult to men. And to me as a single dad! I take this personally. There's an assumption that men are naturally predatory and can't be trusted. I can't square this with real life. Really, you have no idea what abusers are like. I do. I've seen them. It's as though they're from another planet. Their lives are organised around abuse. The vast majority of people are kind and good with motives that are fine and honourable. It's desperately sad that a few monsters have caused all of us to be viewed with suspicion. We need to live in a society based on trust. We're sunk without it.'

'Quite agree. Just can't take the chance.'

Answering back

The boys' head teacher stopped me in the corridor. 'I need to have a word.' We had been walking round the school. I had just been voted in as a Parent Governor and I was on my introductory circuit. 'Be a critical friend' had been the instruction from the training day I had been on. I felt I was performing the duty of the adjective, but that my charm was failing to achieve the noun.

She ushered me into her office. 'I've never felt uncomfortable with any parent in any school I've ever taught at – until I met you.'

That was pretty clear. I had been put in my place. I couldn't quite see why.

'Give me a reason.' I surprised myself with my directness. I was under attack.

'It's your attitude.'

'I haven't said anything yet. Tell me what I've done and I can remedy it.'

Never in my life had I answered back to a teacher. Now I was doing exactly this to someone who was not only a teacher but also my sons' Head. 50 years ago, the word of the Head was the law. My parents brought me to school and collected me from there. Between these times, the school was my world and the adults in it were the law. My parents had absolute confidence in their judgment and, as a child, I was given no reason to question the school's authority. It became a part of our lives and we accepted everything about it without demur. Maybe there was even a touch of gratitude that there were people prepared to educate me. Teachers taught and children learned. Parents received reports. I had assumed I would just send the boys to school, attend the odd meeting with teachers and wait for the reports at the end of term. This institution expected parents to be involved in the learning process in a critical capacity, yet the authority figures in it knew what they were doing and I would have thought the last thing they needed were people like me interfering. In this assumption I was probably right.

'Oh, it's been a difficult morning. One of the parents has made an allegation of racial abuse against one of the pupils. I'm sorry.'

But it could not be unsaid. It had been almost half a century since my last telling-off. I was out of practice and the prospect of being patronised for another three years did not appeal.

Crowd control

'But they're all moving forward.' Ian resisted my hand on his shoulder.

'Well you're not going to.'

The outdoor performance of *Beauty and the Beast* had stopped while the actors lifted away several tots who had encroached into their space, grabbing at the scenery after having good-humouredly barracked them from afar.

'What on earth are the staff doing?'

'They don't intervene,' said the parent at my side. 'They don't see it as their job.'

It's the taking part…

'Ian would love to play a football game. This is something I think he could achieve success at. He needs to have something he's good at doing.'

'No. We don't do that. We don't have winners.'

'I don't think the World Cup would generate quite as much excitement if there were two teams working together to get the job done.'

The Head's mouth betrayed no hint of recognition of the *Bob the Builder* reference.

No winners. No losers. Or, at least, everyone's a winner and everyone gets a 'well done'. No Father's Day as someone might not have a father. Mothers' Day, Christmas, anything that a child might not have or that might be considered part of an exclusive culture had to be viewed with concern and avoided. I knew that a winter tree and winter wishes would not become part of my vocabulary.

*

To the victors, the hugs...

I am unsure what the last straw was. Maybe it was the banning of conkers that had just made headlines in the local paper. Whatever the reason, I was feeling quite tearful most of the time and it had nothing to do with education.

'Just three questions,' I said to the Head of the prep school across the county border. 'Can the children play conkers?'

'Yes.'

'Competitive sports?'

'Yes.'

'And can they embrace each other afterwards either in victory or defeat?'

'Of course.'

'Can you accept them?'

It was so easy. All I had to do was write out a cheque and all my concerns would evaporate. I took another look at the statement I had sent to all the parents in preparation for the election of governors: 'My three sons started at the Infants' School this term. It was a conscious decision to educate them in the state sector rather than privately. High quality education should be available to all children. They are, after all, our future. This will only be possible when parents choose to fight for improvements at their local state school, instead of opting out by writing a cheque to a fee-paying school...

... My boys and I are very happy with the School. I want to make my choice work for my sons and hope I can help achieve the same for all the children at the Infants' School.'

The parents had voted for me. And I had let them down. Within weeks, I was contradicting all my promises and doing exactly what I had said I would stand against. What a fraud I was.

I put the question whether I should change systems to the boys' Head. Correct to the last, she suggested that I would do it and that it would be because of 'public interest'. There had been no public interest in my family arrangements and such a thought had never entered my head, but I removed the boys from the school and resigned as Governor. The Chairman wrote that he thought it 'inappropriate' to ask why.

'Why are we changing schools, Daddy?'

'Because Daddy thinks it best.'

'You don't like Ms X do you, Daddy?'

'Let's put it this way, it's her school and I'm too used to doing things my way.'

'Can we keep our friends?'

'Yes, of course you can. Invite them to play.'

They did. No one came. The old friends disappeared from their lives. I had written the cheque and crossed to the other side. We had entered the world of prep school education, the training ground for the British ruling class.

3

New School

All change

A shiny black Hummer was blocking the drive. Thinking my way clear, I had just turned right across a main road which had been recently declared the third worst school-run in the country. I angled our 10-year-old Renault Scenic across the entrance to enable the oncoming traffic to get past. A small girl in a plaid kilt, her golden hair in ringlets, disgorged herself from the behemoth. She reached inside and extracted a blue bag. Her hand pushed at the door and pushed again. It wobbled slightly. Using both hands she managed to push it almost closed. She pushed again. When a car door is on its first click, it needs to be opened and closed harder to achieve the second. It would be a little while before she learned this fact of life. When she realised it, the monster reared off with a scrunching of gravel. Other parents were stacked up behind me. The main road had ground to a standstill.

I extricated the car from the entrance and entered the drive. Rows of Range Rovers and Volvos had bumped up the kerb onto the grassed verge. I doubted I had enough clearance to avoid grounding. Unable to park, I pulled up alongside the huts that were the pre-prep.

'Welcome to your new school boys. Off you go.'

'You've got to come with us, Daddy. You said you would.'

'OK. I think I can get between these trees. No I can't. Aha!
I'll try in front of the gate to the playground. Nope. That's been
taken up. I'll try going up a kerb.'

In that moment of clarity I knew why four-wheel-drives
were the cars of choice.

Their private school dealt in success. 'There's old money,
new money and snooty money,' I had been told by a parent
when I arrived. 'And there's plenty of it.' Nevertheless, it was
the children who reminded me of what I had come to regard as
normality. As in their state infant school, they were delightful.
Many years before, in a pre-parental incarnation I had a taste of
public school when I was guardian to a boy at Harrow. We sat
in an eatery by the school, looking out onto a pavement
thronged with straw-boatered scholars. We had just been to
Speech Day. 'We've been selective and non co-educational for
hundreds of years' the Head had said to sustained applause 'and
we aren't about to change now.' King Hussein of Jordan had
stepped on my foot en route to his helicopter and my young
ward had, with the wisdom of his 16 years, condemned my suit
as 10 years out-of-date. He was right.

'I love Harrow,' he had said. 'It's the word. You can just
make it last longer. Harrr-ooooh.' It rolled around his mouth
like a fat cigar. 'Not like Eton. That's just too quick. It's over in
a flash. Et'n. It's gone. But Harrr-ooooh. You can make it last
as long as you want.'

'You snob.' I had said at the time. 'Just listen to yourself. If
I have a child I hope to God it won't turn out like you.'

He thought I was joking. I did, too.

My sons were with those who would be assuming the attitudes of those about to leave the prep and move onto public
school. For the school-age me, in the era of post-war austerity,

the people I mixed with knew their place. 60 years on, at this establishment, there was an uncanny similarity. These children knew their place. It was somewhere at the top.

The new regime

I doubted my decision for years. What to do? Pull them again? Pull one – or two? Leave one? How would those who were removed feel? The Health Visitor was all in favour of separating them. I needed to deal in facts. Having dropped the children at school one morning, I paid a visit to the local state junior school. That I had driven from one world into another was clear.

'I haven't got time for this PC nonsense.' The Head was candid. I liked her style. 'Yes, they can win and lose. That's life. Yes, they can come second and third. They can take risks.'

'Can they do French?'

'Only in the last year. It's a pity, but the teaching of foreign languages isn't considered a priority at the moment. It may change.'

'They can do Latin and Greek where they are. I suppose…' The Head smiled wistfully. My voice trailed away.

The children I met were polite and motivated. They reminded me of those I had just left in the car park seven miles away whom they would never meet. It might as well be situated among the outer planets.

I asked the Health Visitor, 'If I moved Ian into the state sector, how would he feel in years to come knowing that I had taken him out of all this because he was having tantrums?'

'You let the antics of a six year old make your decision for you!' he'd say with incredulity and he'd be right.

Ian would get there sooner or later. Lars and Piers would continue to enjoy the challenge of learning whichever sector

they were in. In the meantime, I would live with the hypocrisy
that I felt, both living off and paying to perpetuate that which
I had such reservations about.

Six turned into seven. The pre-prep turned into prep. The
school day was longer and there was homework each evening.
The differences between the boys become more obvious. One
was lapping up all the challenges that came his way. He strove
for success in the classroom and on the sports field and loved
seeing his name at the top of lists of rewards. 'When can I be
a boarder, Daddy?' Another had so imbibed the system of
rewards that he incorporated it into everyday life at home. The
old posters he had placed on the nursery door were consigned
to the bin. Down went the pictogram of a face with an open
mouth and a line through it (the 'no shouting' admonition) and
the one with two stick figures touching each other ('no pushing') on which the inclusion of the names of transgressors had
caused much contention. In their place, a list was blu-tacked to
the nursery door with our four names and columns for credits
and debits, good work and performance awards columns. Some
columns had sub sections with 'DW' ('debit warning') and
'NDW' ('nearly debit warning').

'I gave you a 'PA', Dad, because you dealt with Ian so well.
And I gave Ian a credit for not getting upset.'

Again, it was Ian who had not adjusted to the new regime.

Tears for fears

'I'm really worried about my homework, Daddy. Waaaah!' In the
dim light, I could just see the tears that were springing out and
trickling down his pyjamas. 'It's my Geography. I'll never get it
done.'

'Well, it's General Knowledge, Ian, not Geography and you
will get it done because Daddy will help you with it. But later,

much later. Not at three in the morning. Now, dry those eyes and back to bed.'

The green glow from my bedside clock read 04.50 when the next 'waaah' came.

'My teeth'll fall out. They'll get rotten. My toothbrush isn't long enough to reach them all.' A small finger pressed his jawbone near the ear. 'And there's yellow.'

'Ian, you don't have teeth right up there. What you're feeling is bone, not teeth. And no one's teeth are really white. They're like the story we were reading about the little polar bears. He was worried that he wasn't white and his mum told him to look at all the other polar bears and see how they were grey and beige and yellow and not white.'

'But some are white and some are yellow and some are yellow and white. And the backs'll be black. Give me a mirror. Waaah!'

He snuggled down into the warm cosiness of Daddy's bed and his tiny trembling frame stopped its convulsions. That was what he had wanted all along. I stroked away his tears. He drifted into sleep. I knew that my sleep would not return so I let my mind wander. It was too soon for Obsessive Compulsive Disorder, surely. Yet he was starting to brush his teeth so long that his gums bled. The Health Visitor had asked if these worries were getting in the way of his enjoyment of life. They were. Just the previous day, I had found him hacking at his hair with scissors.

'It'll grow into a tail!' He pulled at the lock of hair that grew at the back of his head. 'And this will grown into a beard!' He tugged at the hair in front of his ears. 'Waaah! Everyone will laugh at me.'

'Then these worries may be a mental health issue,' she had told me. 'Make an appointment with the nurses through your GP.'

Very nice people identified weakness in his working memory and phonological awareness. No, they could not be assisted by the parent. No, they could not be dealt with by the classroom teachers. So complex was this field that I floundered in the terminology – all the adjectivalising of nouns and nominalising of verbs was too much for my brain. The logic behind the provision of support puzzled me, too. Such an expensively-provided service with trained staff in addition to the regular teachers needed to be widely used to justify its existence. I was just not sure if the need was on the part of my son or the service itself. I requested a written rationale of the diagnosed deficiencies – which was promptly supplied – and of the service itself – the questions about which remained unanswered. Chief among these was the need, as I saw it, to remove Ian from lessons I had already paid for and put him in lessons that I would have to pay for again. I also wondered about the difference between the state system whereby Ian would be tested and his specific needs addressed and this system in which his needs would be identified, but would remain unaddressed unless the extra fees were paid.

The Support Counsellor was also recommended for his latent Obsessive Compulsive Disorder.

By chance, I listened to a Radio 4 programme in the car that week. It had the title 'Am I Normal?' It was about working memory, describing, as it put it, 'normal kids having an impaired memory label and being prescribed brain training.' The web site had a link to a working memory test. Ian scored 100%.

I told him to brush his teeth until the gums bled if he wanted to. He did. They did. It was the last time.

'I'm not worried about my teeth any longer, Daddy. Or my hair.'

'Aren't you going to worry about not having anything to

worry about?' Piers enquired, not particularly solicitously. He was right. This normal kid would not be having any brain train-ing.

Botherly love

Having had no sibling relationships myself, I found that life was suddenly being dictated by them. That my sons were relating to each other there was no doubt, but as their behaviour towards each other changed daily, even hourly, I realised only that things were happening, that there were undercurrents of emotion and that reactions tended to be in headline terms and shrieked at full blast. I decided I would be a model of equanimity and not let 'it' get to me, whatever 'it' was.

'Ian's gone, Ian's gone.' Toys were flung into the air and pyjamas were worn until lunch. For the first time, the boys were separated two:one. Ian visited a kind and unsuspecting friend for the weekend and Piers and Lars celebrated on their return from dropping him off with a 'Goodbye Ian Party'. Out came all their toys. 'Ian would never let us do this,' said Lars garnish-ing the chair, piano and floor with Black Beast, Monkey, Sheepie, Bongo Kid, Spidery (the villain of Toyland), Paddington and lots more. Little One could not come. Piers had misplaced him and only wanted to search for him at bedtime.

'These are the events. We're starting with music and games in aid of Ian, well not in aid of him, but because he isn't here and we'll have a dance-off in the den with big books folded out and others on top of them to make a house which Ian would-n't let us do because he thinks we're untidy and he puts our toys away while we're playing them and then we have the 'Get Dressed Timeline', so we start without clothes on and we say this is what the caveman wore and then we put on our pants and say this is what the Aztecs wore, but then some clever ones decided to invent trousers and we keep on putting clothes on until we've put on all the clothes we need. Then we have cool cricket which Ian would never, ever, let us do because he complains about the bowling and says everything's a no ball and he always wins because he's good at it. Then we'll have being kind to the cool cats in which we stroke them and hug them which Ian wouldn't let us do because he thinks Cresta's his and, if he gets Cresta, then Brumas will run away and Pandora will follow him. Anyway, if she's lying down with her claws out she's a bit scary. Then we'll have jumpy javelin in the garden which Ian wouldn't let us do because we'd have to put the javelins back really early in case we hit a bird or dig up the garden.'

'So isn't he protecting the house and garden?'

'No. He thinks it's all his.'

'He wouldn't let us do Treasure Hunt because – because, well, because he wouldn't let us.'

The celebrations began with a gutsy sing-song. Music from their practices at school combined with pieces of pop and Vera Lynn to the accompaniment of whose songs they sang along in the car. 'There'll always be an Engerland while there's a country lane if Engerland means as much to you as Engerland means to me, food glorious food, roast beef and tomatoes and I've been to the year 3000, not much has changed but they live under water and your great-great-granddaughter's fine, she's pretty fine, there'll always be an Engerland and Engerland shall be free if Engerland means as much to you as Engerland means to me-e-e and her ways are ways of gentleness and all her paths are peace and all we ever get is gru-u-el.'

Timetable in hand and newly-bought-from-eBay-with-pocket-money-£5.99-with-postage digital watch on wrist, Lars took charge of ensuring that the events began and ended on time. Wickets became javelins, one of the cats took flight at the prospect of sudden gestures of affection, treasure hunt clues appeared over the house and the three-became-two change of dynamics rolled out over house and garden. The pecking order changed and changed again and I saw for the first time that Ian was, in fact, my little ally, safeguarding the house and keeping his brothers from using household objects in imaginative ways.

'Now it's the art and book-writing competitions and the end-of-the-day poster.'

The boys scurried off with paper and pens and I felt really sorry for the parents of only children. In the novelty of the moment, the brothers were playmates.

'We've done music and games, dance-off in the den, the 'Get Dressed Timeline', cool cricket, being kind to the cats, jumpy javelin, marble boule toystyle, break, keep fit, treasure hunt, toy hide and seek, races, snack, break, gym, poster, book-writing, art and finishing poster. It's been really good and quiet for once.'

The book-writing took the form of stories about 'how much I miss Ian'. Lars took a balanced view. 'I miss Ian because I am so used to being shouted at and beaten up. But we can make more games with three players and Ian is very good at making up new games.' Piers was more condemnatory and put a 'don't' into the title.

'We're like twins now.' Lars's observation was spot-on. It was an unaccustomed dynamic. 'Can we phone Ian?'

Becoming mum

Little One was a fixture on Piers' hand; a constant companion and one whose removal, Ian knew, would reduce its normally placid owner to tears of rage, frustration, hurt or whichever emotion was closest to the surface at the time. Its dark blue knitted shape with two tiny ears and fixed black eyes appealed to his imagination and he became a mouthpiece for Piers' innermost feelings.

'Little One goes to Bear School,' Piers announced. 'He goes there to learn with the other bears, but he'd rather stay at home with me. He doesn't like some of the other bears. In fact, he's going to America to visit his mum. She doesn't live with him, but he loves her very much.' Shortly afterwards, Little One changed his flight plans and booked to go to Africa with Lars's Sweep who was going there to see his family.

The role of the boys' mother when they were five years old was quite straightforward. She was in America. She loved them. They loved her. She was away. These were the facts and they were simply part of their lives. Their mother, or the concept of mother, was hardly even mentioned and, when it was, it was in passing. One or two of the children at school asked about her.

'Where's their mother?' A small face peered up from the paper aeroplane he was making for the boys at after school club. Out of the corner of my eye, I noticed the supervisor's face fall.

'In America. Would you like to see her?' The follow up was instinctive and defensive, designed to stop the questioning at that point. It succeeded.

People were in places. The various neighbours who had become ersatz aunties were in their houses. The godparents were in theirs. The teachers were in school. The swimming coaches were in the pool – or not, if they were men. Everyone had his or her customary place in which they lived out their being. Sometimes they visited or were visited. That was the way of the world. It made perfect sense. Living down a long drive and without immediate family, we did not live in other people's pockets. Visits were arranged in advance and were rarely spontaneous.

'I ruv Ra-fire. He's small. Can he visit?'

Ian knew how to raise his eyes to look irresistibly cute. 'Pleeeeze.'

Raphael was in the year below them and, in a few years,

would probably be too junior for words. At this stage in their pre-prep lives, relations were fluid and, in Ian's case, based on size.

'Ra-fire would like fish and chips, pleeze, Daddy. Or pasta like us. I'll take him to the lavatory. Do you need the lavatory, Ra-fire?' The words were enunciated syllable by syllable.

The word had not yet entered the four year old's vocabulary. Ian tried a variation. 'Toilet? For a wee-wee? Like this.' Ian demonstrated to clarify what he had in mind. 'I think he does, Daddy.'

'I'm sure he'll tell us. Now why don't you take him up to your room and play while Daddy cooks you something?'

It was one of the first 'play days' and, for me, a sure sign of my acceptance as a parent. What mother would leave her child with a single dad unless he were trusted completely? I had become a mum. When the children went to state school, I met plenty of dads at the school gate. They were mainly young. At pre-prep, I met just a few and mainly at football practice. They looked my age. The school gate was populated by mums. Young, elegant, invariably slim and busy mums whose four-by-fours popped out one small child and disappeared.

'Not one bad egg among 'em,' opined a parent at the children's Harvest Festival regarding the line of children presenting their pictures of crops. 'And your nanny?' The statement was interrogatory, assumed that there was one and presumed that she was a 'good thing' otherwise the boys might have been the bad eggs they clearly were not. 'Haven't got one. Not since they were three years old.' 'Your poor wife.' The questioner moved on. 'Haven't got one of those either' was directed at the empty Chanel-fragranced air.

'Ra-fire did a poo, Daddy. Upstairs. I flushed the lavatory.'

'Thank you, Ian.'

'Daddy, Ra-fire isn't eating his cheese.'

'He's a guest, Ian, and guests can do what they want. They don't have to follow the rules.'

'But, if they don't, they don't get invited back.' Lars knew Daddy's view on this subject.

'Got it in one, Lars. But Rafa's doing fine and you're being really solicitous with him. Just like big brothers.'

'He's the smallest boy in the school. That's why I like him. I like small people – and cats.'

'That's very sweet, Ian. We must invite him back. He brings out the best in you.'

4

Swearing

Four letter words

'What's a bugger, Dad? Jack said it. He said 'bugger'. That's what he said 'bugger'.' Piers was determined to get the full value out of this word, the meaning unknown, but suspected to be juicy.

'I'll tell you when you're older. It's a way of saying 'naughty'.'

'But what does it mean? Bugger.' Lars chimed in, relishing the sound. 'Will you tell us when we're nine?'

'Bugger,' Ian echoed. 'I know what it is. It's 'beggar'. That's what it is. It's the same as 'beggar'.'

'No, it's not, Ian. It's something very small.' Piers was thinking through the logic of the word. 'It's small because a bug is small, so it's a tiny person. And he's begging.'

'Something like that, Piers.'

'Jack said 'fut', too, Daddy.' Ian was keen to wring some discomfiture out of this. 'He said 'fut' and that's roood.'

'It's not 'fut', Ian.' Lars was suddenly knowledgeable. 'That's not what it is. It's 'fud'. Oh fud! What would you say if I said 'Oh fud'?'

'I'd say it's time to get up. Into the shower. Hand!' A cupped palm was extended and was filled with green Tesco aloe and teatree shampoo. 'Now smear it on and then fingertips. Do your cootie egg hunt.' Piers' fingers were a blur as shampoo spattered my dressing gown. 'Let me get out of the line of fire, young man. Don't let any of them get away.' With his brothers, it was, 'Harder. You're just tickling them. Get those cootie eggs!'

'S'not fair, Daddy. You always wake me up when I'm in the middle of sleep.'

'Sorry, Ian. That's the way it is with waking up.'

'Dad, I'm seeing a lady. She's helping me with my worries. She is. Not my tantrooms. She's not there to help with my tantrooms. Just my worries. And you can't ask me what we say. It's confirdentshall.'

'I wouldn't dream of asking, Ian, but I suspect she has no idea what you're really like. Do you tell her how angry you can get? Here's the sponge with shower gel. All over. Back of the knees, too. Up your bottom. Everywhere clean and shining, please.'

'Where's my tie?'

'Under your foot, Piers.'

'Where's my trousers?'

'You've got them on.'

'Most ladies dye their hair white.'

'Oh, do they Lars? Why's this?'

'It makes them look as if they like English.'

'So an English teacher should have white hair?'

'If she's a lady. The one at school is 70. Even older than you, Daddy.'

'They call me a mini Mr G.' said Ian. 'They say I look like his son. But they call him 'carrot face'. No, that's not right. They call him 'carrot top'. Don't know why.'

'It's because he's got ginger hair, Ian. Like you.'

'But not like you, Piers. You look like a friend. Lars looks like your mother, Daddy, and I look like you.'

'Piers looks just like his mother's brother.'

'Which one, Daddy? Tina or Melissa?'

'Melissa. She showed me a photo. You're a dead ringer for him.'

'Look at my biceps. I call them Tim and Jill.' Lars said.

Ian had been watching the film 'Kes' after a visit to The Hawk Conservancy near Andover. I assumed he would get more from the scenes of boy and kestrel than from the social commentary of growing up in 1960s Barnsley. Billy Casper, the deuteragonist after the kestrel, punches his drunken brother while getting him into bed. 'Pig (punch), hog (punch), sow (punch), drunken bastard' is Billy's revenge while his brother is comatose with alcohol. Ian latched onto a bird-of-prey reference.

'He called him a buzzard, Dad. Billy called his brother a buzzard. He said 'pig, hog, sow, drunken buzzard.' Why did he call him a buzzard, Dad?'

'Can be a term of abuse, Ian.'

How I wished such innocence might last.

Old-fashioned bribery

As my boys approached their ninth birthday, a wise woman suggested I bribe them with pocket money.

'Half their age in pounds,' she suggested.

The first time they were in a shop with their own money coincided with a visit one Sunday to the local Sainsbury for bread to feed the ducks and swans.

'I want to buy something, Daddy.' Piers was adamant. 'Look, there's Club Penguin membership. Can I buy it?'

'But you're already a member, Piers.'

'Da-ad. Please will you ask someone for *Really Good* Toys for an eight-year-old boy?'

'As opposed to these not-so-good toys for eight-year-old

boys, Lars? Maybe they have a special aisle marked 'Really Good Toys'.'

'Course they do, Daddy. Go and ask someone.'

'You be me, Lars. Let's go and have a look. Maybe it's between the aisle of Really Good Toys for seven-year-old boys and Really Good Toys for nine-year-old boys.'

'Is it?'

'No, Lars. They think all their toys are Really Good.'

So pocket money came into our lives and stayed. It was a potent factor. Any hitting and it was a pound a punch. Rude words were also a pound, but one or two commanded a higher rate.

'You f***ing...'. Piers shrieked as Lars pushed him from behind, sending the toys in his hand flying.

'Right, Piers, that's £10!'

'That's not fair. You saw what he did. You saw it. Fine him!' Piers was florid and trembling at the injustice.

'Upstairs by the time I count to three or it'll be another pound.'

Justice was nothing if not arbitrary. Piers ran upstairs screaming. My audience of two young faces who had been relishing their brother's discomfiture assumed serious looks when my glance turned to them.

'Yes, I know there's a lack of logic.' I was talking more to myself. 'Which is worse, a push or half a word? I have absolutely no idea, but while I'm in charge, it's going to be Daddy's rules – and it's a pound off you, Lars.'

There were times when I missed another grown-up to talk to, get ideas from and, maybe, receive some support from. In the absence of one, I exercised a benevolent dictatorship. Nevertheless, it was the boys who ruled.

5

Birthdays

Party politics

I had brought the boys in early for their fifth birthday party. 'H' was decorating the room. One of guests had already arrived. He came up to me.

'Here's a little something we bought for them.'

My mouth opened to express thanks. It closed immediately.

'Is it for *him*?' H's voice was admonitory – its sudden intrusion into a quiet interchange between two adults intimidating, threatening, menacing. Setting up a children's birthday party must engender a degree of stress, but no one else had arrived yet. The offered present was withdrawn. My outstretched hand dropped down. Both of us felt suddenly guilty.

'It's for the boys.'

'Well, give it to one of *them*.' The crestfallen present giver deposited the parcel into a small hand that turned into six hands, all struggling to rip open the wrapping paper. I retrieved the remains of the gift and put it up high out of the children's reach.

'Oh, no! We want the present!'

'Later, boys. We'll open all the presents at home.'

Lesson learned, but I wondered if the telling-off had been

worth the candle. It was only the first of the afternoon.

H had kindly agreed to host, plan and staff the party. She was the Manager of the children's Nursery School and agreed to rent the premises to me for that afternoon.

'What would you like?'

'Something traditional. Games and party hats. And without the party bags at the end that I certainly don't remember from my own parties in the '50s.' I rather thought she might remember those parties of blind-man's buff and pass the parcel, fairy cakes, blancmange and doilies, too, and that I could safely leave the arrangements to her.

'Leave it to me.'

I agreed without demur. She was the Manager.

'And how many cakes and what type? Just bring the boys along and they can say what they want.' Or rather the immediate thought that is going through their heads at that particular moment, I said to myself. Nevertheless, involving the children in the planning was another rational proposal, so I happily agreed to this, too. The bustle of everyday life with three simultaneous and different agendas does tend to chip away at the memory, however. Having agreed to bring them up the following week, I promptly forgot and remembered only a few days before the event.

H's banter was not characterised by subtlety. 'Thought you'd died. Too late now.' But she elicited what their current thinking was. Whether they linked what appeared on the day with their expressed preference, I have no idea, but H was satisfied that she had achieved a child-centred choice. While I was there, I took the boys to see the staff they had been so fond of before they had left to go to the 'big school' that infant school was at that time. The names on the drawers were different; the photos on the coathooks had changed. Nothing was as it had been. They, too, had moved on and they knew it. A month is a long time in a five year old's life.

'Hello, boys. My how grown-up you look in your school uniforms!'

Each boy squirmed.

'Come on. Say hello. You've been dying to come back and see everyone.'

That was quite true. They had been excited at the prospect of returning. The reality was clearly something else. They clung to my legs and peered sideways at the open arms presented to them rather than have the cuddles from the Nursery staff that they had welcomed and been so used to just four short weeks before. It was the end of yet another era. Nursery was now a venue for their birthday party, nothing more.

Private parts

'Who's making all the noise?' The party guests were frozen into statues at the pause in the music. The look was accusatory. Several parents involuntarily clapped their hands to their mouths. There was instant silence from them, too. It was my fault. 'Tell the parents to leave their children and come back at five' had been my instructions. 'We've got staff. We know what we're doing. Parents just complicate things and some of the little ones will run to them rather than join in.' She was right again. One of mine had done exactly that and was giving an impression of being a limpet.

'Daddy, I don't want to play. There's too much noise. I just want to be with you.'

'That's part of the fun. Look, Ian, everyone's come to see you.'

'But there's too much people.'

'Come outside for a couple of minutes for a breath of air. It's much when it's quantity and many when it's number, by the way.' Years of EFL teaching had left their mark.

Ian let the difference between countable and uncountable nouns pass. 'But I'm tired.'

'Come on anyway.'

'It's too cold.'

'OK. Let's go back and see what your brothers are doing. There may be prizes to be won.'

'It's too hot.'

It was just as forecast. Should I leave my own party and go shopping? What to do for the best? These dilemmas were quite new. A mother whose son had been a friend of my three came up to apologise for not having been in touch since the last party.

'I'm getting married in the summer.'

'That's nice. Someone you know?'

I was saved by the arrival of three cakes in the shapes of a car, a lorry and a doggie. Candles blown out, the guests drifted away. 'No toys, please' had been the request on the invitations. Over a hundred books and games were piled into plastic bags. Bedtime stories for the next few years were assured.

'It's Little One's birthday today. He's five, too.' Back at home, Piers held up his knitted blue glove puppet. 'You're my Daddy and I'm Little One's Daddy. I have to look after him because he can't do anything for himself. He goes to Bear School when we go to school.'

'Does he learn anything?'

'Well, I don't know, but he doesn't get any bigger.'

'If your hand gets bigger, he'll stretch.'

'But he can't move on his own, except jump.'

Piers threw the toy in the air.

'He's like the Velveteen Rabbit I was reading to you, isn't he? He hasn't got any legs.'

Piers looked doubtful as he put the puppet on his hand again and wriggled his fingers in the stumpy arms.

'He hasn't got any *hind* legs.' I was duly corrected.

Piers was backing towards the lavatory. Unlike his brothers, he would avoid using public facilities, often waiting for hours until he could use his own. Maybe his not wanting to wee-wee standing up had something to do with this.

'That's what I meant. I should have been more specific.' I glanced at his steady backwards progress to the open lavatory. His brothers had just been there. The seat was up. The child's plastic insert had been taken off and lay on the floor. 'Oh, come on, Piers. Do it like a boy, for a change.'

'No. Don't want to.' His hands flapped as they did when he felt he might be thwarted. His smile was beatific. 'I'm going to wee-wee. I'm going to wee-wee sitting down.'

'But you just make life difficult for yourself...' My mouth remained open. Maybe I could have intervened just a moment sooner. Did I secretly want him to experience for himself the perils of not doing things the boy's way? It was to be the highlight of a very long day. Feeling the backs of his knees touch the porcelain, Piers bent himself at the waist, sat back – and disappeared into the pan. Smugness gone, a small finger wagged from the depths.

'And you can stop laughing, Daddy.'

The trials of age

'S'not fair and s'all your fault. I'll never get used to being nine. I've just got used to being eight and now I'm nine and I'll never remember it, Daddy.'

Lars was more practical than Ian. 'It's not fair that you have to go to school on your birthday. You shouldn't have to when it's your special day and no one else bothers. When I'm in public life, I'll make a law that you have a holiday when it's your birthday. I will, Daddy.'

Piers peeled a '9' from one of his cards and stuck it on his school pullover with no comment.

Battle royale

And another two birthdays after this…

'Just our friends. They're the only ones we want to invite.'

Lars was quite right. It was their 11th birthday party, no one else's. They should invite whoever they wanted. Why couldn't I leave it at that? That was the logical decision, right for a child of that age, and simple to arrange. A small birthday party. Looking back, I should have listened to them, but no, I had to know better.

'What about the moral high ground?'

'Where's that, Dad?'

They had no idea.

'Well, you remember when we went go-karting and happened to see half the boys in your year group there and then we knew that we'd stumbled on a birthday party you hadn't been invited to?'

'Yes. They were the cool guys.'

'And you remember that I said that it was small-minded and petty of them not to have invited you?'

'Yes, but we didn't care. We don't like them. They're horrible.'

'And I also said that we would never be small-minded or petty?'

'Yes. So what?'

In truth, I had admired the boys' insouciance and the absence of discomfiture of the parent who had organised the go-karting miles from home and who had never imagined that any of those not invited would have simply happened upon it by chance. My sons cared not one jot at being excluded. So why should I care? What right did I have to impose my own sense of what is morally right on anyone else? But I did. It was wrong and I felt I should take a stand against it.

'I'll write out invitations to all the boys, give them to you and you can decide who to give them to.'

'Oh, don't do that. We don't want to give them to people we don't like.'

'Well, that's your choice. My take on it is that, just as we thought there was something wrong in their not inviting you, we shouldn't also be in the wrong by not inviting them. Anyway, I guess that those who don't like you won't want to come anyway.'

Off went the invitations with a deadline, so that I could get a 'thank you for coming to our party' gift printed, and back came the replies – several after the deadline. A laser party with guns that showed tracer lines, with smoke and with sound effects, was too exciting a prospect to miss out on. Almost all the cool guys decided to come.

They all seemed like charming young men to me as I greeted them at the door. Parents disappeared, promising to return in two hours. The gifts table was piled high. Everyone went into a briefing room. The lights dimmed. A smoke machine filled the air with the fog of war, just like the freezing variety outside on that February night. The battles began.

Green and red tracers illuminated the darkness. Pop music drowned the sound of laser rays. Shadowy, blurred figures stalked each other in the gloom. 'Kill', 'hit', 'bring 'im dahn!' It was *Lord of the Flies* time. The prep school veneer cracked and vanished. I sat in front of a hardening mound of crudites and sandwiches, provided for the parents who chose to stay, with the sole other grown up and watched 23 pre-teenage boys slug it out emerging sweaty and fulfilled two hours later.

'Happy birthday to Pierwwwrriannnars. Happy birthday to you.'

And it was all over. Whoever had been victorious out of the three teams, each captained by one of my sons, I had no idea. That a great time had been had, I was quite sure.

'I don't care about the moral high ground. Whatever it is, it isn't worth having.'

The atmosphere in the icy blackness of the car on the way home was as cold as the frozen rain dripping from the leaden sky.

'They showed no respect. It was my special day and they didn't bother.'

'Who didn't bother?'

'The cool guys – I told you they wouldn't appreciate it. You spend all that money on them and they don't care. They don't like us and they don't respect us. There was no point in inviting them. You're so kind and they're so. So…'

Lars broke down in tears of frustration.

'One of them knocked him off a wall he shouldn't have been climbing.'

'Maybe that's coloured your impression.'

'No, it hasn't, Daddy. You've got all these ideas of how people should be nice to each other and how we should be nice to them, but it was OUR party, not yours. We didn't want them. You did. But you didn't have to play with them. Not again, please, please. They're horrible and disrespectful and don't appreciate anything. They don't appreciate you like we do. We just want our friends. We don't want the moral high ground. It's not worth having.'

I had been told. I had just received a practical lesson in how the theoretically morally right comes unstuck in reality. How I was quite wrong to put my moral philosophy in the way of my sons' happiness. In the fullness of time, they may well see that I was right, but who am I to tell them how the world should be? It is unjust, unfair and has its share of children who may grow up to be delightful, but who should be allowed to spend their early years in the company of those who are as unpleasant as they are.

'I'm sorry. I just wanted to do what I thought was right.'

But that was wrong. There I was putting guilt on them for not enjoying what my clumsy attempt at social engineering had spoiled for them. The other parents had it right all along. They just let their sons invite who they want. I should do the same and let social conscience take a break. No more mass invitations. No more high ground. Sauve qui peut!

'I'm sorry, Daddy. I really enjoyed the party.' Lars's face, puffy and red-eyed, peeped above the duvet.

'I know, Lars. I know.'

'It's just that I love you so much and they don't care. And I know what you do to try to make us happy.'

6

Godparents

Religion was entering the boys' lives for the first time. At state infant school, the emphasis was to avoid offending anyone about anything, probably not out of kindness or consideration, but as part of their risk aversion – the ultimate risk being litigation. Rather than talk about God as '(s)he' and attempt to embrace all religions while maybe running the risk of forgetting one so recherché as to have just one believer, the concept was not raised. It was different at pre-prep.

Although I had decided to have them christened, this was at a time when my parenting skills were a repeat performance of how I had been parented. In those days, being christened was simply the next big event for a baby after being born. As part of my push to have them made British citizens, it seemed logical for them to be welcomed into the Church of England. The local vicar embraced the idea of three small additions to his flock and gave me his full support. Christening = godparents = aunts and uncles. My lack of brothers, sisters or wife had deprived my sons of an extended family. With a christening, I had the ability to create an ersatz and quasi-official one out of friends. The sole proviso was that I attend christening classes.

These resulted for me in a damascene conversion as powerful as Paul's in the opposite direction. Nevertheless, the boys became officially C of E. Matters of doctrine cropped up from time to time.

'If the Baby Jesus was dead, how did he come back, Daddy?'

'Well, he wasn't a baby when he died, but that's what the Bible says.'

'But YOU said that when our cat, Claudius, broke his leg and died that he wouldn't come back because he was dead. AND you said that our grandparents were dead and that we'd never see them. But the Baby Jesus went to heaven and came back.'

'Some people believe this, yes.'

'If you believe it enough, then it becomes real – like the Velveteen Rabbit. Is that what you're saying, Daddy?'

'Not quite. What I'm saying is that it may be true and some people really believe it is. It's to do with God and, because we have very small brains, we can't understand what He does.'

The 'if He exists' remained in my head, unspoken. It was complicated enough already.

'They tell us, 'Give a man a fish and he'll eat for a day. Teach him how to fish and he'll eat for life.'

'How true Piers.'

'He'll need a fishing rod, though.'

'And I know about Fathers' Day, Daddy. It's the day Jesus did everything for his father.'

Doctrinal discussions tended to be brief.

Ian looked at what his brother was drinking. 'May I have some Early Grey tea, too, please, Daddy?'

Quick to spot the slip, Lars rejoined with, 'It's Earl Grey. It's lovely. It tastes of nothing.'

Feeling left out, Piers chipped in. 'Daddy? You know you go red when you're embarrassed. Your penis flips up, too.'

'May I leave the table?' said Lars.

'No,' said Piers. 'You can't leave the table unless you're Ian –
who is sitting on it. You can only leave the chair.'

Ian pushed his empty plate towards Lars.

'Ian, do they teach you to do that at school?'

'No, Daddy. I learned it on my own.'

'At school, they call me Liar Lars. I'm going to tell a lie now.'

'Are you, Lars?'

'No. I lied.'

'But it *was* a lie,' said Piers. 'You said you would tell a lie and
you lied.'

'Do you like your job, Daddy? Looking after us. You have to
look after us. Then you die.' Ian brushed my cheek with his
hand. 'When I'm old,' he announced, 'My skin will fall off and
this will be underneath.'

'But if you sit somewhere for a very long time, you get black.
Like 10 days,' said Piers.

'No,' said Lars. 'It's 20 days.'

'We'll be 10,' said Ian. 'After 10, we'll be… let's see…
Monday, Tuesday. No. January, February…'

'There's some food on your face, Ian.' He dropped his cheek
to his shoulder and wiped it across his sweater. A fragment of
doughnut lay trapped in the fibres. He put his mouth to it.

'Don't worry, Daddy,' said Lars. 'When I have my children,
I'll visit your grave.'

But not all the Godparents saw eye-to-eye with me as I was
to discover.

Christian kindness

'I don't agree with what you're doing. Dragging them off to
America.'

The lips were puckered; the eyes averted; the head shaking
side to side and the back stiff. Belinda pulled her cardigan

around her as protective armour against what verbal assaults I might be about to hurl in her direction. I was reminded of a disapproving woman in the audience of the 'Esther' programme the year the boys were born who gathered her skirt around her as she spoke lest some of the contagion seep from me to her. I smiled at the recollection.

We were in the kitchen. Belinda-and-Jonathan were a double-act. I had known them for the best part of 35 years since I used to teach their son. They had been on the Parents' Committee at the school and many was the evening we had ended up to the elbows in soapy water at the kitchen sink after a Bring and Buy or whatever event. Their friendship with me remained long after their son had left the school and our only common interest had disappeared. Every year my birthday was remembered. I provided the car at their son's wedding and was invited to dinner once or twice a year. Jonathan helped me secure the mortgage I needed to build my first house. When I told them my plans for a child, they were unfazed. 'You told us 20 years ago you might do something like this. We're not surprised.' Their memory was better than mine. It had been a last resort in the back of my mind not, I had thought, an idea I externalised. In the last few years they had become devoted to a young Indian girl, the daughter of people who owned a restaurant they visited and, in the absence of a real grandchild, had become honorary grandparents to her, having her overnight and taking her on holiday. They were kind and loving and seemed an obvious choice to take on a special role for the boys. I could not choose one over the other so they became a caring unit. When I popped the question about a special involvement with the children, their initial response was that they were too old.

'Come off it, 70's the new 50.'

They took little persuading. I offered them a choice of child.

There was no hesitation. Piers it was to be.

They were dutiful beyond expectations. Every visit was accompanied by thoughtfully chosen presents – a garden swing, a tricycle, whatever was right for that time. The other boys received bags of gifts, too. I was sure they enjoyed the choosing and giving as much as the boys enjoyed the receiving.

'We were just at the hobby shop and saw this.' See-through flashing key-fob fish were handed to each child. 'We thought they'd like these.' Six eyes lit up as the toys came out – a tiny quivering ladybird in a wooden box for Ian ('We know how much he likes animals'); an early reader for Lars; a cuddly toy for Piers. Clearly, any time they went anywhere they had the boys in mind and if they spotted something appropriate, stored it away for the next visit.

'I wonder what Auntie-Belinda-and-Uncle-Jonathan will bring this time.'

'Now boys, you mustn't…'

'Expect anything, so you won't be disappointed' they chorused. They had my stock answer off pat.

'And you mustn't expect anything anyway. People come and you enjoy them, not what they might bring.'

The children loved their visits. It was with them that they had their first outing to a restaurant. 'Ugh, Daddy. It's just yucky.' Marco Pierre White's risotto, like many of the less predictable dishes I tried on them, was pushed to the centre of the table. Piers was the ideal choice as he, like them, was ever so slightly 'proper'. They took him to their hearts.

'Will I go to a sleepover with Auntie-Belinda-and-Uncle-Jonathan, Daddy?'

'Could well be, Piers. When you're a bit older.'

They had come with presents for the boys' fifth birthday. Belinda did not know what to look at. She examined the kitchen furniture. There was no eye contact. It was the first critical comment I had received from them, or anyone.

'Not sure that I'm actually 'dragging' them anywhere. It sounds as though they're screaming and protesting. They're quite happy about going and seeing their mother. In fact, were it not for the BBC, I doubt I'd have managed to find their mother. I've tried to locate her myself, but haven't been able to. Anyway, I haven't signed the contract yet.'

'Maybe we're just not the television generation, but why do you have to let them be filmed?'

'Well, I don't have to, of course, but the BBC isn't about to find their mother for our benefit. They want a documentary out of it. I don't know where their mother is or how to find her, so if the BBC is willing to use its resources to do it, I'm happy for them to go ahead. I think it would be really good for the children to be in contact with her. Anyway, let's find out what the boys think. Boys…' I called them in. 'What would you say if I told you the filmmakers were coming this afternoon?'

Their faces lit up. 'Oh yes, Daddy. They play with us.' Films of Record who were making the documentary for the BBC's 'One Life' series employed a young crew. The two cameramen and young PA had come to know the boys well, generally during a rumbustious hide-and-seek.

I looked at Belinda. 'I think that says it all, don't you?' The lips tightened. Clearly she did not.

'Well we're going to have to agree to disagree, aren't we? I don't think it's such a big thing.'

The rest of the day went as usual and we waved goodbye to them. I forgot about the event.

Like it or lump it

'We haven't heard from Auntie-Belinda-and-Uncle-Jonathan for such a long time.' Piers was wearing his puzzled face.

'Yes, it must be the best part of a year.' Earlier that year, in March, I had received no birthday card for the first time since I had known them. 'Oh dear,' I told a friend. 'Belinda's cross with me. I hope it's not one of her feuds.' When I first came to know her, she had fallen out with a neighbour, uttering not a word to her in 23 years until the day she died. While the source of the disagreement became lost in history, the passion took on its own momentum. 'That would really be a pity.'

The spring and summer passed without contact. Although the presence of Auntie-Belinda-and-Uncle-Jonathan had disappeared from our lives, their names came up in conversation as the boys tended to ask who had given them whatever book or toy they were playing with at the time, and they had been exceptionally generous.

'Maybe they don't get out much any more,' I ventured. 'They aren't as young as they were.'

As Christmas approached, I wondered if the feud – for that's what it seemed to be – had spread to their special charge. No card; no present. It had.

Surrounded, as they were, with cards and gifts, the boys did not notice. Nevertheless I included them on our list of those for whom the boys would draw cards and buy small presents. On Boxing Day we were due to visit a godparent who lived nearby, so we took the gifts with us to drop them off. The boys were full of Christmas down to their Santa Claus hats. I tried to prepare them for the reception we might receive.

'Now, boys, we haven't been invited and aren't expected, so it's almost certain it will be a very quick visit just to give them your cards and the little pot plants. Some people don't like being taken by surprise, so we may not even be invited in.'

I have always told the children, 'If you can't say something good about someone, don't say anything at all,' but I wondered if there might be a perverse pleasure in seeing appropriate toys and not buying them, in denying oneself what must have been a joyful experience in order to express, even if only to oneself, righteous indignation. I dismissed the thought. Life's too short.

The house seemed empty when I rang the doorbell.

'Not in, boys, we'll just leave everything in the porch.' There was a movement behind the glass. 'Oh, Belinda.'

The door opened. There was no facial acknowledgement that she knew us.

'We're expecting friends.'

Was it my imagination or was there a stress on the last word in that sentence so that whoever was coming was and we were not?

'We were on way to Uncle Ian's and thought we'd just drop off some things the boys made for you.'

'You'd better come in.'

Inside the sitting room door, the boys burst into chatter. 'D'jwanna know what we had for Christmas?' Fortunately without a pause, they just launched into a breathless list of their presents, finishing with – 'And we had costumes for Batman – and Robin.'

'And I had Superman.' Piers swished his cloak, rustling the lights on the Christmas tree.

They looked into Belinda's face for a reaction. They looked in vain. The stare was blank and uninterested. The silence needed to be filled.

'Well, boys, we must be off.'

'Yes, you must.' Jonathan, who had left the sitting room as we entered with the words 'You can't do this, Ian', had walked round to the front door and stood holding it open.

'Lovely to see you. Bye. Say bye bye, boys.'

'Bye bye Auntie-Belinda-and-Uncle-Jonathan. Bye bye.'

'Now boys, as I said, they don't like being taken by surprise, but you behaved very well. Let's get on the road for Uncle Ian's.'

Not a word was mentioned about the visit which had lasted all of three minutes. On a road I knew well, I found had taken a wrong turn. When we eventually arrived at Ian's, there were people we had never met. The welcome could not have been warmer.

Two months later, it was the boys' sixth birthday. There was no card for Piers. He wrote a note hoping that they would be able to come to their birthday party the next year. Their birthday coincided with half-term and we were visiting friends overseas so I asked them to post it. At least it might not end up straight in the bin.

At about this time, Christopher Wool's print 'House' came up at auction. I put in a bid for it and, until the boys started to read, it hung on the kitchen wall. The boys could make out most of the words, but such is Mr Wool's way with graphics, that there was one word that was unreadable, or almost so.

'If you don't like it you can get the'… don't know what this is… something 'out of my house.' What's the 'something', Daddy?'

"Hell'.'

'But it begins with a 'fff'.'

'Can't imagine what it is, then.'

7

Holidays

Chalk and cheese

'We've been doing 'avertising' at school, Daddy.'

'That's nice' had become the standard instant reaction to anything that was apropos to nothing at all as many of the boys' opening gambits had become. The rhetorical 'what on earth are you studying advertising for at five and a half?' was more directed at me than at them, but it was there to be picked up on.

'But it's really interesting.'

'You surprise me. How's that?'

'Because,' Piers piped up in that slightly exasperated tone of having to state the obvious, 'I want to know what people are doing with them. Some are making pies and some are making crumble and some are drinking them. That's appletising.'

'Oh, it's about apples, is it? But what if people had bananas in their kitchen?'

'Then that would be bananatising, of course.'

'And pears?'

'Peartising. Don't be silly, Daddy.'

'Are we nearly in Texas?' Lars asked from under the pile of bedding that was part of a self-catering holiday.

'We're not going to Texas this time.'

'No, silly, we're going to the seaside. Are we nearly in Sandy Aygo, Daddy?'

Memories of their visit to America some months before were still fresh in their minds. The last time they had seen the sea was the blue Pacific in San Diego.

'It's very sandy there. Is Cornwall still in Engerland?'

The sea appeared as we rounded a corner.

'It's the same as the sky.' As both were grey, this was said with Eeyore-like resignation.

'We'll play 'I-Spy',' said Piers. He flapped his hands like the chorus in 'The Black and White Minstrels Show', a sure sign that he was hatching a clever ploy. The Matchbox Batman Car (Batmobile was too long a word at this stage) had been confiscated partly as it was an item of contention and partly as it had been denuded of its rubber tyres which left four sharp metal wheel rims free to gouge whatever skin or surface it was whooshed along by small hands. 'Here are the new rules. Whoever thinks what I'm thinking gets the Batman Car.' After a brief pause to let this sink in and in the absence of a response from his brothers, he continued, 'I'm thinking of the Batman Car, therefore I get the Batman Car because no one guessed it.' Another pause. 'Don't I, Daddy?'

'I spy with my little eye, something beginning with 'g'. I won. I won. It's the sea.'

'That's 's',' said Lars, perceptively.

'No, it's the grey sea.'

A sign marked the entrance. 'Duporth Holiday Village.'

'Here we are boys.'

'I want to go home, Daddy.'

I kept the 'so do I' unsaid. 'Here's our holiday home for the next week. We'll find where our chalet is and then see the sea.'

'Do we have to?'

'Yes.'

Happy campers

Momentarily, I had no idea what on earth I was doing there. I had not enjoyed the family holidays at Duporth. Its mix of compulsory fun and games were of little appeal to this quiet and bookish boy. I could not logicalise the antipathy so said nothing. My parents loved it and, every year from the age of five until I was 17, woke me up at three in the morning to start the drive down the A303 to St Austell in Cornwall. Most of the journey was in a queue following a caravan along single carriageways. After 12 hours in the back of a 1939 Austin Eight which had a permanent whiff of carbon monoxide, 'Can we see the sea yet?' was more a plea than a question. Duporth was a holiday camp. The absence of 'wakey-wakey' Tannoy announcements and redcoats marked it out as upmarket, genteel even. In the days before cheap flights and package holidays in the sun, this is where the doctors, lawyers and other professionals would take their families for their standard two week holiday. The accommodation was in chalets. These were basic in the extreme – one-roomed asbestos huts containing one or more beds, each with a 'guzunder' in case of a night time emergency, a jug and a washbowl on a chest of drawers. That was it. Lavatories were in a separate block, along with wash handbasins. There were no showers, but a bath could be booked in the Manor House, a huge, crumbling pile in the grounds, whose bedrooms commanded a premium and whose billiard room was hung with heavy velvet drapes faded by decades of sun, the merest touch of which sent myriads of particles into the shafts of sunlight that streamed through its milky windows.

How enormous were its rooms and how heavy its doors to this very small boy in the mid-1950s who occasionally absented himself from his parents and their troupe of friends to savour alone its welcome quiescence and shade, filling his nostrils with odours, albeit of damp and decay mixed with nicotine, quite different from the briny of the beach and the disinfectant of the communal facilities. There were knockout competitions like quoits and cork 'n ball. The latter involved throwing a tennis ball at a cork in a white circle on a green wooden square board. For those who were more sedentary, there were afternoon tasks, like creating a garden on a tea tray. Intelligent adults would busy themselves for hours creating small landscapes out of earth, stones and heather for prizes like china Duporth thimbles or cigarette boxes. While my parents signed up for cork 'n ball, table tennis, or shove ha'penny and while little girls and their parents created miniature gardens on tea trays with flowers, paths marked out in tiny sea shells, and mum's make-up mirror serving as a pond, I wandered round the site in my own Enid Blytonesque world of smugglers, wreckers and spies.

Scavenger hunts and other children's activities were entrusted to a petit lady in late middle age whose short back and sides, lovat jacket and dark tie gave a severe aspect; a tight corset keeping her spine in place contributing to her upright demeanour and sudden, unbending movements. Later I discovered that she had been in constant pain. I was never sure about Auntie Wyn and, indeed, there was no reason for her to warm to this dour child who, in all the years she worked as social organiser, became animated only once when he spelled 'Majorca' correctly in public and was rewarded with a five bob prize. One year I noticed her absence and was told she had killed herself.

As I grew up, I was occasionally allowed in the ballroom ('take your partners, please, for the valeta') and could join in the nightly housey housey. To this day, I can remember all the rhymes for the numbers and can do a mean wolf whistle after 'legs eleven'. I wondered what the 'doctor's orders' for a number nine were, but assumed they were something adult and unmentionable. Meals were at set times at set tables and there was no deviation from the fixed menu in which 'Windsor Soup', a thin brown liquid, frequently featured. Evenings could be formal with jacket and tie or cravat or special with vice-versa shows and fancy dress parades.

Within this regimented framework, campers formed real relationships during the one or two weeks of their stay. Even for me, after the first few days the bonhomie eclipsed the essential tattiness of the surroundings. There was a walk each day, either spontaneously to the beach down a steep footpath flanked by high, moss coated walls the constant damp from which trickled into gullies, the water discharging at the side of 30 steep concrete steps which led to the beach, or organised ones along the cliff top to Charlestown and beyond. The start of a meal was announced by the blast of a steam whistle, pulled by a child as a treat for being especially good. Grace was sung:

'Always eat when you are hungry.
Always drink when you are dry.
Close your eyes when you are sleeping.
Don't stop breathing or you'll die.'

For anyone arriving after grace had been sung, a penny was to be put in the late box.

In a post-war Britain used to rules and being told what to do, no one thought twice about an eleven o'clock closedown to the strains of 'Goodnight campers, I can see you yawning. Goodnight campers, see you in the morning. You must cheer up, or you'll soon be dead, for I've heard it said, most folk die in bed, so I'll say goodnight campers, don't sleep in your braces, goodnight campers put your teeth in Jeyses. Drown your sorrow, bring the empties back tomorrow – goodnight campers, goodnight.' In this cloud of euphoria, everyone drifted back to their chalets and went to bed. Photographs of the time show me in a clip-on bow tie and aertex shirt between my father in a cravat and my mother in a floating summer dress of her own creation. While my parents mixed easily with their age group, establishing instant holiday relationships and swapping wartime stories, I was left to my own devices.

Occasionally, I found a friend, related with intensity and was left devastated when we all went home, never to meet again. Knowing that this would inevitably happen, I mooched around, missing my dog, my room and my friends at home, counting the days until the end. When I was 16, I achieved some independence by having my Lambretta brought down by train and, when I was 17, my father was quite happy to let me take his swish, black MG Magnette round the coastline. That was the end of the family holidays. For the next 42 years I had no desire to return to Duporth; hardly gave it a second thought. Then, for no conscious reason, into my head came the knowledge that I had to take the first holiday with my own family there; the same place, the same week in August. I toyed with the idea that, just maybe, I might find people to jog along with in the same way as my parents had all those decades ago. I typed 'Duporth St Austell' into Google and found a planning application to redevelop the site. Scrolling down the list, I saw that their latest web site was years old and phoned on the off-chance. They still existed and, yes, they had an entertainments programme for children. Back in the 1950s, bills were payable by the last Friday of your stay. These days, it was by credit card in advance. I paid up and wondered what other changes might have happened in the four decades since I had last set foot there.

*

The times, they are a'changing

Preparing for my first holiday in 42 years bore little resemblance to the preparations my parents had made. I employed an 'animal angel' to live in the house in our absence, partly to look after the cats, but also for security. A note was put on the business web site that there would be hiatus in activities. Along with toys, I popped the boys' three laptops and a selection of DVDs into the car and we set off mid-morning. Maybe they would enjoy in their childhood what I so memorably had not in mine. Even though it was a Bank Holiday Saturday, we arrived before five in the afternoon and hunted for our chalet.

The Google search had hinted that Duporth had seen better days. Compared with 42 years earlier, it had also seen worse. Bayview 2 was to be our home for the next two weeks. We could park in front of it, unheard of in the 1950s when the few cars that campers had were consigned to far-flung fields. It was a semi-detached, three-roomed wooden hut that was showing signs of disrepair but had not been built when I had last been at Duporth. Its en-suite bathroom and loo would have been the height of indulgence in 1964; its kitchen with cooker, fridge and microwave unheard-of; its TV an unnecessary distraction from the entertainments programme. Yet there was a shabbiness that announced the place was on its last legs. Repairs and renewals needed to have happened five years before. Duporth Holiday Camp had died of a lack of sophistication and been re-invented as Duporth Holiday Village whose clientele was now drifting away. In post-war Britain, people worked at having fun and, to a large extent, made their own. Not now. The main adult entertainment was bingo. For the rest of the evening, the notice-board showed the photos of cabaret artists; a far cry from the shows that made use only of the campers' talents. The 21st-century Duporth visitors were just passing through. And whatever their professions might be, doctors and solicitors they were certainly not.

'That man's got earrings, Daddy.'

'That man's got a ponytail, Daddy.'

The boys were merely observing. They had rarely seen either before and wanted me to share the experience.

'What's that lady got?'

'Those are tattoos, darling.'

'Why?'

'Good question. I suppose some people think they look nice.'

The small nose wrinkled in disapproval. Beauty was not in the eye of this beholder.

'And I think I needn't say this, but I can tell you, boys, that if you ever have any of those done, you'll be disinherited on the spot.'

We were waiting for the children's activities to begin. Paul was in charge. He had been a cabaret singer. The background music in the 'Dolphin Club' was him singing. His voice was like velvet. 'It gives me accommodation, you see.' I was the only parent in a room full of youngsters aged five and upwards. 'They use this as childcare,' Paul told me. It was an observation with no criticism implied. As the customers were involved in a writing activity which was a stage my three had reached only recently, we moved over to the ball park carrying a '5s and under' notice located close to the one-armed bandits in the amusement arcade. The boys squealed with delight at this unexpected facility, dived in and on each other, hurled balls around and clambered onto the padded sides. The writing activity came to an end; a massive child with an incipient moustache pulled the netting aside and slid down the plastic cladding. Piers flapped his hands, greatly exercised at this intrusion into his world. A few seconds later some other large children arrived and flattened him under their weight.

'Come here, Savannah.' The helper was pointing at a nine year old with make-up, earrings, high heels and a handbag.

'Let's go, boys. Enough's enough.' We moved off towards the path that led to the beach. It was a path I had last trodden 42 years ago. The boys ran ahead down the steep incline, trailing their fingers along the soaking walls, jumping in and out of the gullies, shrieking their anticipation of the sea, 'Hang on, boys, let me capture this on film' uttered to the empty air.

'Crabs!'

Six feet squelched down the concrete steps, past the huge rocky outcrop with tufts of grass onto the coarse sand and shingle of the beach. My young self, for years a photographic memory in black and white, skinny against a grey sea, was now standing in my mind's eye pink with maroon trunks, slim against crashing breakers, utterly alone and vulnerable. I blinked away the image and saw instead three confident little boys, each armed with a fishing net, heading towards the crabs and shrimps in the rock pools. 42 years. Two generations. The beach – identical. Everything else – changed beyond belief. I have always looked younger than my years. At that moment, I felt rejuvenated and, through my sons, experienced the vicarious thrill of boyhood – never so fulfilled.

There was the massive grass-topped boulder at the foot of the steps that had been cut by prisoners of war three-quarters of a century before. Lars immediately climbed it. 'This is my place, Daddy. You'll always find me here.' Shale was piled at the foot of the cliffs as before, but now with danger notices. Until the tide went out, the shore was rock and shingle. The smooth sand was visible by courtesy of the moon twice a day beyond the rock pools.

The beach became the focus of our stay. No one had uttered more than a 'Hello' or an 'Are they triplets?' to us during our time there. The camaraderie had vanished. The easygoing acceptance, the desire of the campers of decades before to subsume themselves into a community, replaced by a hard-edged self-interest, a grim determination to have fun on one's own terms.

In the early 1960s, the ballroom and dining area were burned to the ground and replaced by a curved concrete complex with huge windows designed to resemble the prow of an ocean liner. The dramatic white linear structure stood out starkly against the Velasquez blue of the Cornish summer sky. It was new when I last saw it. Now, its windows bricked up, its rendering coming apart, it was a hulk awaiting the scrap yard. The old manor house had disappeared, its grounds of exotic semi-tropical trees and banks of hydrangeas now a wasteland. Maybe Duporth was already doomed when I was there as a child. The mateyness that my parents' generation so readily accepted seemed just bizarre to me then and a touching relic of the past now. The 'camp' was no more. It became just a place to stay. The secluded beach remained the draw. It was where my father taught me to swim, where I ran up and down in an imaginary world and later where I first savoured the delightful pain of calf love. I felt a tug at my hand.

Waves were breaking around the rock pools as the sea entered them. The sun was setting and we were about to leave, hoping the boys would snuggle down and sleep the journey away. Three buckets held sea creatures and shells.

'Can we come back, Dad?' Lars looked earnest, pleading. I could never have imagined this scenario 42 years ago. Nor could I have imagined my answer.

'Oh, yes, absolutely.'

We never did. I had seen short visits to Duporth being part of our summers for years to come. It was not to be. I had chosen to return just in time. 2006 was its last season. After that summer it was demolished and a housing estate built with just two of the 1920s chalets preserved to show what it had been. Another chapter in my past had closed and the world moved on.

8

Hitting

Lars' fables

In common with most parents, I assumed that if you brought children up with moral values in a loving environment, they would respond in kind. The hypocrisy of hitting children for hitting others was clear enough. How could I tell a child that hitting is wrong and punish by doing the wrong thing that was the cause of the punishment in the first place? Children learn quickly by example and a single parent is a de facto role model.

With two of the brothers, this clearly became a truism. Lars and Piers asked me to fold a few sheets of A4 and staple them into a book. Off they went happily to write such works as 'The Rood Man' – whose eponymous hero sported a speech bubble 'Shut Yer Gob' – a phrase learned from a classmate whose parents owned much of Berkshire. He came to a sticky end when those around him rejected him. Lars's books ended with 'by Lars M.' and a list of his other titles: 'Also by Lars M.'

'You think you're a famous writer, Lars.'

'I am.'

Ian's writing was of a different nature. 'Slof the Sloth' was a collection of drawings with sentences around them.

'Read it to me, Daddy.'

'Tess the squirrel and the fox...'

'No, Tess is the fox. You can't read it properly.'

'Ian, you start writing on the left and continue to the right. Then you carry on below what you've just written. If you start at the bottom right and work upwards, it's so different from everyone else that people won't understand you.'

'I'm an idiot.'

With a single movement of the hand, the book was pulled apart. Lars and Piers carried on with their writing.

'Waaah.'

The mouth was open and salivating; the face crumpled into a florid puffball of tears and snot.

'You don't want to do that, Ian. I'll fix it for you.'

A hand swung into my face. Lars and Piers were transfixed. Daddy had been hit. That was something right outside their experience. Mine, too. There was more to come.

'You're...' Arms and legs flailed while a suitable killer adjective was sought. 'Pooey!'

Piers' book was thrown to the floor and Lars pushed on top of this. So far removed was this behaviour from the sweetness and reason that had characterised their early years that I was slow to respond. A leg shot out and Piers was down.

'Up you go, young man.'

Transformed into a writing melange of arms and legs, all aimed at causing injury, little Ian was conveyed to the nursery.

'Won't stay. Wanna come down. Waaah. I'll hit you.'

'You'll stay up here and think about it. You can't hit your brothers. You can't hit Daddy.'

'Yes I can. You're pooey.'

'You'll spend some time here on your own, thinking about it.'

'I've thought about it. I want to come down.'

'You'll think about it some more.'

'How many minutes?'

'Four.'

'Waaah. I only want three.'

In the event, it was more than half an hour, but as Ian had no idea about time, let alone how to tell it, he didn't notice. Lars and Piers remained occupied with their reading and drawing. When I called Ian down, they tensed, waiting for an attack.

'How can I be good, Daddy? I'll never be good. Waaah. I'm sorry, Daddy. I've hurt my only Daddy. I've hurt my best friend. Waaah.'

'You've got to try harder. You can't go around hitting people. Look at everything you're good at. You know more about animals than Daddy ever will.'

'I'm a camera. It's up here. Did you used to think this when you were a postman?'

Years before when we had been climbing Beacon Hill, I pointed out to the boys where Daddy had ridden his bike through the grounds of Highclere Castle when he had been a postman briefly during a university vacation in 1968.

'How on earth do you remember this? That's amazing, Ian.'

But lurking in the background, almost but not quite unspoken, was his secret; a secret that revealed itself every day; a secret that he knew everyone knew and that, now that he was in Year Two, had to be confronted and articulated. Compared to his two brothers, his reading, writing and use of numbers were way behind.

Quiz whizz

'I think he's the cleverest, but in an unconventional, unacademic and entrepreneurial way. He's also a good two years less mature than they are.' The Head of the pre-prep eased herself back on her chair. 'How would feel about his starting Year One again?'

'That'll make him different. On the continent, many coun-
tries don't start their children at school until they're seven.' I
still wanted all my boys to have the same happy childhood that
had been my privilege in the 1950s, to learn by playing, just to
pick up skills as they developed. 50 years on, it was a more pressurised world. 'You told me yourself that their brains aren't
fully formed until they're seven or so. It will all come. Maybe it
will just take time.'

'I only thought that he might feel better about himself if he
were more grown up than the other children in his class and
doing work that he could cope with.'

As a child, learning had come easily to me, just as it was for
Ian's brothers. This was new territory. Logic told me that I
should accept the views of the experts, but being a parent was
also teaching me powerful lessons.

'Daddy, I read this in Year One.' The book was flung down.
It was contemptible, to be viewed with disdain. This was not a
book to be re-visited in Year Two. I took a look at the stamp
inside it. 'Reception.' He had been on books a year below his
chronological level even then.

'Must be a mistake, Ian. Tell you what. Why don't you have
a go at the book Lars is reading.'

Ian admired Lars. 'Ian wants to be Lars because Lars is a
writer like you,' I had been told. Lars fetched his book from his
bag and Ian turned the pages.

'I can't do this. The print's too tiny.'

I put a finger under the first word.

'Tuh, huh, eh. The.' There the familiarity ended. The next
was a word with more than four letters. By splitting words into
syllables, Ian managed several pages, but he knew the truth as
well as anyone. No matter that his general knowledge would
have won him a place on any quiz programme or that his
memory for events could rival that of a savant, it was the skills

of literacy and numeracy that were prized. For his brothers who played daily with numbers and letters, it was a joy to succeed. For Ian, it was a constant reminder that he was deficient. For his Daddy it was a question of dealing with the compensatory behaviour that would follow.

9

Birds and the Bees

The notion of 'Mummy' hardly featured in their lives. When the word was used, it always related to Melissa. Although English Law did not recognise It, she was their mother. I could see her in each of the boys. When we met in 2006, Melissa brought some photo albums. She showed me a photo of her father, a man some years younger than me, the boys' maternal grandfather. 'He's a biker,' she said fondly. The picture was of a man with hair to his waist and tattoos all over his arms.

'What does he think about your creations?'

'I haven't told him.'

I felt sure that Melissa's parents would be proud of the grandchildren they didn't know they had but did not press the issue. This was Melissa's decision. I know that, had I been her parent, I would have been saddened to have been denied this knowledge.

In preparation for meeting Tina and Melissa, I had covered the 'egg and seed' aspect some weeks before as I thought I should at least attempt some explanation as to why they had two mothers. I had started it before boiling the eggs for breakfast.

'Look boys. What's this?'

They stated the obvious and waited for the more that they knew would come.

'Something like this comes from a mummy. When this is washed in seed, it's fertilised. Then it's put into a mummy's tummy, and after a while a baby comes out.'

They had been unimpressed.

'Not a chicken?'

A few days later, I expanded on this when I was drying them after their shower.

'And this is where your seeds come from to fertilise the egg.'

'Can we fertilise the egg, Daddy?'

'When you're older. Not yet awhile.'

'I don't think there are seeds in there. It's two meatballs,' added Lars.

As the years went by, their comprehension became more sophisticated, if not more accurate.

'If I do a wee and see some seeds, I don't want to flush them away. It's such a waste.' Piers was adamant.

'All those children drowned in the sea,' Lars added. 'How do you know you've got seeds?'

'You make an educated guess,' I replied.

'Did you only have three seeds, Daddy, and no eggs?'

Melissa's role in all this was comprehended vaguely.

'Why doesn't Melissa have the same name as us?'

'Because we aren't married. She was married to someone else. She donated her eggs. I hadn't met her when you were born. Now she's become unmarried.'

Piers thought about this. 'When you stop being married, they give you your old name back, don't they? Do you have to give your children back?'

'Piers, you love the idea of someone being in charge, making decisions for you, but there's no 'they' to give you your name back. You choose.'

'But doesn't the government have to allow you?'

'The Government doesn't have a hand in any of this. Yet.

People can make their own choices. This is what Melissa did. Let's hope that we can stay free to make our own decisions. Given half a chance, the Government would involve itself in more and more aspects of our lives. The most important thing is freedom, boys. The price of freedom is eternal vigilance.' I was starting to lose them. 'OK. What I mean is you can't take freedom for granted. You have to treasure it and stand up and shout when you think it's being taken away. In this country right now, you can be who you want to be. You don't have to prove who you are. I do hope one of you will go into public life and fight for our freedom.'

'I want to go into public life, Daddy.' Ian was quite serious. He had been the only one to go into the Public Gallery of the Scottish Parliament with me and hear part of a debate which happened to be on child protection. The subject matter was unknown to him, but what struck him was the formality of the language and structure of the debate – how educated speakers could call into question each other's veracity in the most urbane and polite language, how a question could be answered when none of the facts was addressed and how the Speaker could assure the Members that the Minister had used the opportunity to answer the question while clearly he had done the opposite.

Motorhome mania

'I want to be a policeman, Daddy.'

'Piers wants to be a policeman so he can tell us all what to do.' Lars understood his brother rather well. I had asked them to tell what magazines they would like me to subscribe to. Ian was already receiving the BBC's 'Wildlife' every month.

'Police Gazette.' Piers had no doubts and was undeterred by its non-existence. 'Why isn't there one?' he had demanded of the newsagent and promptly started writing his own.

'Motorhome Monthly' was Lars's choice. This did exist and he had the odd copy, although I would not take a subscription to something that was more for the retired than for children. He became enthused about the various makes and wanted me to sell the house and move into a Winnebago. When on the road, the appearance of anything that resembled a house on wheels needed to be registered.

'On Wednesday… RV… we're playing away at Cot Hill. You can pick us up… caravan… at five thirty unless you come to watch the match… caravan… but if you do, we want to go back in the bus… RV.'

Whether it was a journey with the family or a school trip, the verbal nervous tick was the same. His classmates persuaded him to say 'A' instead. When we passed the Caravan and Motorhome Show at the Newbury Showground, the 'waaaah!' he exhaled at my refusal to stop rivalled the 'Horrid Henry' show we were en route to seeing.

Motorised caravans and procreation shared a bizarrerie.

'When there's an old mother and she dies and you marry a young mother, is she my mother-in law?'

'No, Piers, she's the mother of your husband or wife, if you marry.'

'But I thought they made you marry to have children.'

'No one makes you do anything. You can choose.'

'But if you have triplets, they have to be the same, don't they? Anyway, I want to be an only child.'

This was something they all agreed on.

'I like going to the doctor, Daddy. That's when I can have Daddy time all on my own.'

'Do you have to leave home when you marry?' Lars asked. 'Look! There's an RV towing a caravan.'

'By that time, I expect you'd want to.'

'No, I always want to live with you,' Lars replied. 'Does that mean that if you married, you'd leave us?'

'If we had a mum,' Ian looked serious 'She'd have to go. Did you marry Melissa?'

'No. She was already married.'

'Is she in love? Do they kiss? On the lips?'

'They used to, but she's separated now.' I anticipated the 'why'. 'Sometimes people grow apart.'

'Do they have to give their children back then?'

'Oh, that's all quite complicated. It won't happen to you.'

'You won't have to give us back?'

'There's no one to give you back to, is there? Don't worry.'

'But if say the mummy marries again, then that's a new family and the child won't feel right in it, so she would have to hand the child back to the daddy, wouldn't she? Because you can't have one weekend in one family and the next weekend in another family, can you? You wouldn't know where you are.'

'Many do, Piers, but I'd've thought the most difficult thing is having the two people you love most in the world not able to stand each other.'

This concept was off their radar. Their experience of grown-ups disagreeing was almost nonexistent. Piers thought for an example he could relate to and came up with sleepovers with his former nanny.

'When we stay with Auntie Clara, she shouts at Uncle Nigel. They seem quite cross.'

'That's how some grown-ups are with each other. Daddy can't very well argue with himself, can he?'

'Dad.' Lars looked intense. 'If I saw you walking down the street, I'd know there was something different about you. Not just that you had three sons. It's because you're kind and good and... and... well, you're my Dad. I love you so much. You're the best dad a boy like me could have.'

'I hear there are some very good dads on Planet Zog, Lars.'

'Even better than them, Dad.'
'Why are your eyes wet, Dad?'

The one and only

Although Mummy was hardly ever mentioned, for me, there was only one, Melissa. The boys also knew they had met Tina, who gave birth to them, although their perception of her was hazy. She became confused with Toni who had a similar physiognomy and who used to prepare meals at their school. Melissa's name was firmly imprinted in their minds. Her photograph stood by the stairs for them to see every night before they went to bed. She worked with children's charities looking after deprived children, yet had no wish for children of her own.

She e-mailed me shortly afterwards: 'I went to lunch with a friend today. She told me a friend of hers had seen an article about me being an egg donor in the *National Enquirer* (of all places). I told her I had not seen it but I looked on-line when I got back. I did not find the article but I found comments on it on one site. Most of what they had to say was not only cruel but untrue! It's so awful – and they mention where I work, which makes me very uncomfortable. I wish people would educate themselves a little more – and use more reputable sources than the *National Enquirer* before they post or publish these kinds of things.'

I commiserated: 'You and I see things in a very similar way, Melissa. We are maybe more pragmatic than some, but things will change and what we have done will seem quite mundane in a few generations' time. I quite understand your shock at reading what people you have never met and who have no knowledge of you can say about you.'

She replied: '*National Enquirer* is an over-the-top tabloid magazine with scandalous and gossipy stories. People consider the magazine a joke and I shouldn't be offended by what they or a random stranger on the Internet may say about me but I was just shocked when I came across it yesterday. I guess it just hurts when you try to be the best person you can be and all of a sudden you come across criticism that makes you out to be a cold, heartless, selfish monster! I feel a lot better now, though. I am glad that you have had a positive response. Some people still seem to think that people and their lifestyles should fit into some tidy, pre-defined box in order to be 'normal', 'proper', and 'acceptable'. I am glad to know that through your books, appearances, etc., you are showing people that quite simply, love is love and family is family, even if it comes brimming over the edges of that box – or bursting through the seams! I am happy to see you and the boys sharing a wonderful, loving life together. That's what it's all about!'

Depending on your viewpoint, my sons had either two mothers or no mother at all. At any rate, none was around for them. I was it. Both. All. The lot.

'What's the official line on their mother?' One of their classmate's parents was nothing if not direct.

'She's in America.'

'Just that?'

'That's all there is. She 'is' in that she exists and she is 'in America'. That's the truth and that's exactly what the boys know. In fact, that applies to both their mothers.'

Try as I might, however, I simply could not see Tina in them – mainly because she was not in them, not in any way at all. She was fantastic in that she gave birth to them, but there the connection stopped. There was no more. No genes, no blood. They had nothing in common with her. She was incredibly brave. I could not have done what either of them did. I could neither have walked away from my own children nor have seen children to whom I had given birth as anything other than my own.

Being an only child and a single parent, I became used to the idea of being 'it' so far as Piers, Ian and Lars were concerned. A visit to the grandparents is a visit to the cemetery. Effectively, the boys have no relatives apart from me. For years, I assumed this was a fact.

When my contractual relationship with Tina finished, she assured me that she would not do it again for anyone else as it could, as she said to me, 'never be so wonderful again'. With these words, I congratulated myself on being the ideal client for Tina and for Vivian, the agency owner who introduced me to Tina originally. They must have thought so, too.

A few years after the boys were born, I had a telephone call from a man who opened the conversation by telling me that, although we had never met, he felt a special connection between us as our children had shared a womb. Quite how that related my sons to his twin daughters and, by extension, him with me, I was not sure, but I was curious to hear his story. I gathered that Vivian had told him how well my 'procedure' went, had recommended Tina and that Tina had decided to go down the surrogacy road again with another single man, coincidentally also called 'Ian'. The procedure had not been quite as smooth as mine had been and Tina had ended up with a hysterectomy. 'You're better off without it,' she was told.

Ian was keen for my boys to meet his daughters and, as he was travelling to England, he included us in his itinerary. His daughters were delightful. He was charming. My boys were too young to understand the connection and, try as I might, I could feel no link at all. In fact, it just brought back memories of a time best forgotten when I was doing something that was alien to me and which could have ended in tears. My life BC (Before Children) might as well have been just that. It seemed a lifetime away. I was completely used to being a Dad and operating in

Daddy mode. There was no blood tie between our children; his reasons for having children by surrogacy were different from mine; there was no point of contact. We parted amicably and quite possibly permanently.

I assumed that these girls had been carried by Tina because Vivian considered me to be one of her success stories. I gave it no more thought but, if I had followed this skein through to its logical conclusion, I could have imagined the other scenario that was to follow – Ian Mucklejohn and family, the sequel. Vivian would take the starring role, as surrogate; Melissa would give support as donor. Who would be the director?

When I was in San Diego, I would meet him.

What the dramatis personae in my story did with their lives afterwards was not for me to know, nor was it of particular interest. The 'job' had been done. Our connection was over. We would exchange greetings at Christmas and keep in touch, but that essentially was that. We moved on. It was on a visit to California with the boys when they were six that Vivian told me 'You know they have half-brothers? Would you like to meet them?'

I had no idea, but being in the United States and in the company of those who had held my hand for the earliest steps on my journey brought back to me the surreality of my sons' conception. I was less surprised in California to know that the process had not ended with me than I would have been in Berkshire.

'Yes, of course,' was my response. 'I knew that Melissa had donated eggs in the past, but I thought those I had were the only ones that resulted in a pregnancy. She must have donated after me, then.' Vivian nodded.

It was to be a family gathering. Into my motel room, came Melissa, Tina and Vivian. An additional person entered; a stooped and elderly man in jacket and regimental tie. I focused on him. Who was he? 'Hello, you must be the grandfather,' was my automatic reaction as he was clutching the hands of two small, handsome blond-haired boys. I assumed he had come to take them away at the end of it all. 'Or great-grandfather,' I thought. I extended my hand to be shaken. He relinquished the hands of the boys who went off to play with my sons. The man introduced himself to me by name. He was clearly 'old school'; out of kilter with the rest of the assembled group, differentiated by age, formality and a dossier which he proudly showed to anyone who came by while buttonholing them and, ancient-mariner style, delivering a monologue about his life and times. The collected papers included pictures of himself during the second world war and a photocopied obituary of his wife. I was to be the wedding guest of Coleridge's poem and I was, indeed, to rise a sadder and wiser man the morrow morn.

The elderly man took my hand and shook it. 'Nope. I'm the daddy.' He motioned to the three-year-old twin boys who, as they were products of Melissa, were my sons' half-brothers. 'He was born without an anus.' A paternal hand stroked a blond head.

'Poor little chap.' Sorry as I was for his physical deficiency, my comment was to encompass his whole being – and that of his brother. The daddy was 81.

81 and solely responsible for two small boys. He had become a single father at 78. Vivian had arranged it. She had taken the role of surrogate herself. Melissa had acted as donor. I could see Piers in both children. No wonder I had been considered suitable. I wondered who might be seen as unsuitable. This was changing everything. Could it get any worse?

'The sperm was surgically removed.'

It could.

Here was an old man in every sense. Although his small sons clutched him round the knees and called him 'Daddy', I could see no other point of reference that he might have with them. He had been young during the war, long before I was born. My own father would have been just 17 when he was born. He spoke as in a rehearsed soliloquy, without pause, as he handed out his documents, his credentials, clearly assuming that his audience was fascinated. I was transfixed. This was altogether too much information. He would brook no interruption, would not break off after every couple of sentences to see if there was any 'co' in the conversation.

My head reeled. The small all-American boys tucked into coke and crisps. My three were on orange juice and fruit. They played on the floor with toys, British and American accents intermingling. They had no idea of the family connection that I had just discovered.

Melissa had brought some photo albums. She opened the page at a picture of her brother as a child and put the flat of her hand across his nose and mouth. She did the same to a picture of her as a girl, her hair in bunches. Everything still exposed was Piers. 'And I was obsessive about symmetry,' she was saying.

'How bizarre.' I replied. 'Piers was very upset the other day because the characters on his Winnie-the-Pooh plate didn't line up with the edge of the table. I thought he was bonkers, gave him a plain white plate and told him not to be so silly.'

Slowly, these people I hardly knew and could now hardly believe left. The room fell silent. I closed the door and felt my heart racing. My head was in my hands. I sank down onto the bed.

'Fuckin' 'ell' came the Essex accent of a friend who was helping entertain the children. 'Is he the father?'

I needed to reflect. We went to a diner.

'That's what you get in an entrepreneurial free-market society,' was the waiter's comment on our conversation. 'If you can pay for it, you can get what you want.'

He was right. I could and did. The elderly man had simply done the same.

'Who am I to judge?'

'Well, you're nearly a quarter of a century younger for a start.' We were back in the hotel room. 'And there aren't any checks on parents getting together the conventional way.'

'I'm really floundering. What's the difference between giving nature a helping hand and doing something utterly unnatural? It's all subjective. Of course the authorities could step in if the children were in danger or neglected, but just as money can buy whatever process is wanted, so it can buy legal opinion to counter any action.'

'So what's your point?'

'It's just that he's a very elderly parent.'

And it was also just that something so shattering had happened that I could not get my head around it. Whatever can these people have been thinking? I had related what I had done only to me. I knew that I was right. By all empirical standards that was still true. There were other people who thought it was right for them. And they were utterly wrong. I was being judgmental and I was right to be so.

My friend looked at me critically. 'You could be 39.'

It helped. I felt incredibly young in comparison, switched on, in tune with my children, old enough to be responsible yet not too old for atrophy to have set in. I didn't look my age or feel it. Should my not having been in a relationship have precluded me from doing what I did? Of course not.

Nevertheless, I had my doubts. By looking at a distance at a situation like mine, I had seen the selfishness that is a huge part of surrogacy and what I saw was not a pretty sight.

'Don't beat yourself up about it,' my friend said. 'You love those boys and they love you. They're happy and well-adjusted. They love their lives.'

'But I've seen what I did, stripped down to its basics. Selfish parent; vulnerable children; huge risk.'

'That's what life is. You have to trust yourself that you're the right person to create life. You did. You are.'

And then there were almost four...

'We've seen us.' Lars was emphatic in front of his teacher. He paused so that the specialness of his words would sink in. 'When we were pies.'

His teacher was nonplussed. She mentioned it to me casually at their prep school's staff-parent evening which I generally referred to as a staff versus parents match.

'Oh yes,' I said. 'That's what they looked like when they were embryos. I've put a photo of the three of them when they were embryos on their nursery wall. This must be the earliest ever family photo. That was Lars's first reaction: 'We look like pies.' The expression has stuck. He's right, you know, they do look like pies.' Thereafter, Lars would often refer to the past before they were born as 'When we were pies.' He says, 'The war was on when we were pies, Daddy.'

I doubt if their teacher had ever contemplated the visual similarity between an embryo and a pie and was possibly taken aback by my jocularity. I had long ago lost all sensitivity to the mechanics of their creation. The photo of the embryos was one of the marker points in their creation and I was happy to show it to them. It was one of the first scans sent to me from the IVF clinic in La Jolla to help me realise that events were moving ahead, and it had an other-worldly pale blue sheen to it. The four discs could just as easily have been flying saucers.

In terms of the 'Ben 10' and aliens science fiction that Lars was into, such primitive space machines were so unsophisticated that I doubted if he had ever encountered the term. 'Pies'

had a boyish straightforwardness to it that appealed to me. I
needed to doctor it first, though, as the photo showed the four
embryos that were implanted into Tina. I often wondered what
happened to number four and what that child would have been
like. Did it just die or was it subsumed into the surviving three?
These were questions to which I had no answer and I did not
wish to be asked. It would introduce a note of sadness into
what I saw as an essentially happy and fulfilling story. Doing a
Stalin and re-writing history with some early cutting-and-
pasting, I took a pair of scissors and trimmed out the bottom-
most pie. Maybe the one I excised was one of the three.
Perhaps the deceased one – for I now saw these pies as mini
babies – was among the three on display. It was crude but
expedient and it worked. I knew that someday I would tell
them the truth about the fourth pie, but imagined that would
lie in their teenage years. The truth came out when they were
eight.

I had not reckoned on the ubiquity of YouTube.

'You said we'd be with you for the rest of your life. That's
so nice.' Ian ran up to me. 'And that we had little fingers and
toes.' The words seemed familiar, although I was sure I had not
used them to him.

'Where did you hear this, Ian?'

'On YouTube. You were there.'

They had been looked after by someone with no knowledge
of computers who had been impressed with Ian's dexterity on
the keyboard and the assuredness with which he looked up his
own name on Google. Assuming that he was about to see a
baby film of himself, he had clicked his way to the site and saw
not his former self, but his Daddy talking frankly to a camera.

'Come. I'll show you.' He moved his hand beckoningly
towards the small study where their laptops sat.

Lars was in tears. He ran to me, burying his head in my

stomach. I pushed a hand through his wiry red hair.

'It's so... so...' He was hunting for the mot juste. 'Nice.' He dismissed that choice. 'Lovely. Loving. We'll be together for the rest of your life. But I don't want you to die, Daddy.'

Piers, too, was in floods. 'Oh, Daddy, Daddy...' What had I done? Was this the moment that the tabloid journalists had foreseen when the children realised the dreadful truth? Not so. These tears were outpourings of joy.

A picture of me from a couple of years earlier covered the computer screen. A woman using sign language was in the foreground. They had the hard-of-hearing version of a film I had made for the Equal Opportunities Commission – 'Equally Different.' It had never occurred to me that my children would find out about their background that way. My words came back to me. They were simple and they were from the heart. I was saying what I felt. It was not how I had imagined telling them of their creation, but in three minutes and 34 seconds and complete with subtitles in Welsh, they had the elements of their story with images of their birth mother, biological mother, grandfather, and themselves, right from the day the film was shot when they were six back to being embryos. I couldn't have put it better myself – and it was me who was doing all the narration. It was both tender and matter-of-fact. It set the tone for my reaction to their reaction.

'Gosh, I'd forgotten all about that. Clever of you to find it. So that's the story.'

'But we could have been four. Quads. What happened to the fourth one of us? Did he die?'

'Quite possibly, but this one was only a tiny speck and it often happens. I'm just so happy to have you three.'

I put my arm around all of them.

'It might have been a girl.' Ian spoke with a hint of regret, whether because a sister would have been a preferable addition or because he was at the stage of regarding all girls as silly, I chose not to explore.

'No it couldn't.' Piers was adamant. 'Because triplets all have to be the same.'

Later, at bedtime, Lars looked into the large mirrors which were the folding doors of the nursery wardrobe, contorted his features and started sobbing. 'I want the other brother, Daddy.' Through the bathroom mirror, I could see him, one eye on his reflected performance, practising wailing. 'No you don't, Lars. Two brothers is plenty. It might have been a sister anyway. Piers isn't always right.' Realising that he was getting nowhere with this line, but keen to continue the melancholia, he reverted to a familiar theme. 'I always want to be with you, Daddy.' Red-eyed, he climbed up the ladder to his top bunk.

'Lars is crying because of the ways.' Ian said, darkly.

'"The ways"?'

'It's because he's thinking of what's going to go away. He thinks that everything that's good will go away and that he'll be sad.'

10

Illness

Telling it like it is

'How are you today, Ian?' The voice at the other end of my mobile phone was someone unknown, cold-calling about business.

'Just been diagnosed with cancer a couple of minutes ago.'

There was a silence. I let it continue.

'I don't know what to say.'

'You asked, so I told you. If you hadn't wanted to know, you needn't have asked the question.'

Generally, in response to a casual query about my welfare from a complete stranger drumming up business, I would answer, 'Still able to write a cheque.' Even from people I know, this is a question I find difficult to reply to, mainly, I suppose, because either no response, or 'fine thanks' is all that's required, but I view the world through glasses that are sufficiently rose-tinted to hope that the enquirer may actually care. I can cope with 'How do you do?' as this is a traditionally understood rhetorical polite greeting, the reply to which establishes whether or not you are aware of social niceties ('How do you do?') or not ('Fine thanks'). 'All right?', 'You well?' or any of the variations that just possibly may, or more likely will not, mean what they say will generally elicit from me a noncommittal 'Functioning, thank you.' When I was growing up, enquiries about one's welfare were uttered only when there was real concern and they were never meaningless. In this more brittle, modern age, they are about as close to concern as one is likely to get.

That time, I knew just what to say. I should not have done it. It was so cruel that I never did it again.

It was also true. It made me question seriously for the first time the wisdom of what had seemed so positive and uplifting in 1999. I thought I might die and leave three very young children with no one to care for them.

Ever since I could remember, I had a mole on my right shoulder blade. It was the only mole on my back and it was quite large. I hardly ever saw it and never paid it any attention. I am not a sun-worshipper. It was commented on by no one. It just sat there, ignored.

Not having been to the doctor since my mortgage application in 1975, my visits to the surgery with the children for vaccinations and minor injuries were novel events. Having little else to occupy myself as we waited, I scanned the posters. The picture of a melanoma struck a chord and I remembered my mole. The one on the wall was mottled and bleeding. I took another look at mine. It was just the same. Nevertheless, it was a biggie, so I made my first appointment in 30 years and lifted my shirt. Cool fingers stroked my back.

'Outline looks nice and regular, but it's large, so I'll get a colleague to photograph it and we'll see if there are any changes.'

Some days later, I lifted my shirt once more for the doctor with the camera. She was not so sanguine and suggested there would be no harm in removing it – immediately. Within 24 hours it had been sliced off. A few days later, I was at a private clinic with a grey-haired lady in front of me telling me that it was malignant. My days as a person had ended. Not only had I become a patient, I had become the condition.

As a person, you can choose who touches you where. You can choose to be clothed or not. You can choose who gets close enough to hurt you. It's different as a patient. The surgeon put his serious face on and went through the possibilities. There would be scans, x-rays and a blood test to see if it had spread. If it had, chemotherapy would follow. If it had not, there would be a 'wider excision' to remove skin from around the original melanoma which would be sent for tests. Cancer. I had never thought about it, let alone considered for an instant that it might touch my life. But there it may be, waiting. In my organised life, here was something out of control, random, capricious. It was a new and unwelcome intrusion that might tear me from my sons. What would become of these tiny orphaned children? Financially, they would be provided for. I had even insured against inheritance tax robbing them of their home. But how could I stop this thing, this excrescence, robbing them of their father? A mole, of all things. A brown mark.

'We don't know why they can suddenly become nasty. In fact, all we really know is that melanomas have to be cut out. They're on the increase and you'll have to watch out for the sun as you're fair-skinned. Your boys, too, if they have the same skin colour.'

I could feel the cancer spreading as he spoke, consuming skin, circulating through the blood, hitching itself onto every innocent organ I could imagine. I was poked, prodded, scanned and tested. That I was called in after a few days to be told that it would be a wider excision after all was a huge relief. It would mean a day in hospital. For the first time, I would not be able to conceal the truth from my sons. Something was wrong with Daddy and, sooner or later, they would know it.

*

The C word

Many years before, I had a 13-year-old boy from Beirut on one of my Courses. In the early hours the telephone rang and woke me. His parents were calling me to tell me that there had been a car accident and that the boy's brother had been killed. They wanted me to make arrangements for the boy to come home as the funeral was to be the following day, as was the custom in the Lebanon. This call was almost immediately followed by another. They decided not to bring the boy home. They decided to have the funeral without him and tell him about his brother's death when he came home. For the rest of the boy's stay with us, the parents kept up the pretence that his brother was alive. In their telephone calls to him they told him that his brother sent his love. Every time the boy went on a trip, he would come back with a small gift. 'It's for my brother,' he would tell me.

When I said goodbye to him at Heathrow Airport, I knew that in the space of a few hours, this boy's world would be turned upside down and he would know that a terrible truth had been kept from him. Would he trust his parents again? How would he feel about having been lied to? I wrote him a letter telling him that, by the time he received it, he would know the truth. He would know how brave his parents had been to let him have a wonderful time rather than to bring him home and spoil his summer when there was nothing he could do about the tragedy that happened to him. I did not believe a word of what I was writing. He came back the following summer. The moment he saw me, he burst into tears. I put my arm around him. 'I know,' I said. 'I knew.' At that moment, I decided being open with children was the only way to prevent the long-term hurt that must come from the mistrust that would follow being lied to, even if there was nothing they could do and even if it hurt. Their ability to trust a parent was all important and it was up to the parent to present this truth in an acceptable, supportive and undramatic way. That I would tell them was a certainty. How to tell them was more parlous. I decided to be matter-of-fact and direct.

'Daddy has to have some skin removed from his back, boys.'

They accepted this information without comment.

'He'll be in hospital on Friday and he'll be a bit tired when he comes out.'

'Will you make our dinner?'

'I think we'll just have a pizza.'

'Goodeeee!' Their enthusiasm was far greater than if I had offered to do a four course cordon bleu feast.

I thought I would introduce the dreaded 'c' word just in passing.

'Daddy has had a sort of cancer removed and the doctors need to know that it hasn't spread.'

'And if it has?'

'Then we may have a problem, but we'll take things one step at a time. OK?'

'OK, Dad.'

And that was that. At that point, the idea of cancer had been introduced. In my childhood cancer equalled death and a rather nasty death at that. For them, cancer was removable, treatable, liveable with. They would grow up in the knowledge that Daddy had had or even had cancer and that, palpably, he was still alive. There was just the operation to undergo.

'Just let me insert this suppository…' The nurse held a coloured phial and approached me with intent. I declined and requested a DIY option. 'And take these pills orally.'

I had been warned not to make any serious decisions post-operatively, but managed to decide what flavour pizza to give the boys for their supper, wash them, put them in their pyjamas and cuddle them goodnight.

'What's that, Daddy?'

What I had thought was the mixture of sweat and adrenaline in the small of the back that had become second-nature after a day being chief cook, bottle-washer and everything else that a single dad takes on board, was a pink trickle down my legs. The wound had opened. The boys screamed at the stab-mark in Daddy's back. I wrapped towels around me in a tourni-quet, dropped some more on the floor to blot the small pools, talked the boys through the difference between blood and other secretions and searched out the 1001 for the carpet. Over the next few days, anyone who came to the house was likely to be asked to remove the sodden dressings. No longer was I the one in charge. For the first time since being a baby, I felt dependent. Grateful though I was, it was an unaccustomed and undermining experience. Always I had been able to count on myself. Now I had to confront my own mortality. Way back I had learned the joke about the meaning of the word 'indis-pensability': plunge your hands into a bucket of water and take them out. The hole that's left is your indispensability. But I *was* indispensable. The boys had no one else. There were no blood relatives, no doting grandparents and, while there were godpar-ents who would nominally act as guardians, there was no one who loved them as I did.

I looked into their open, trusting faces. 'You always have each other, boys. You are each other's best friends.' I knew this was true, but they were at the age of squabbles and 'me first', of the need for instant gratification and of tantrums which, although they were no longer of the lying on the floor banging fists and feet variety, were of universal proportions. They loved each other deeply, touchingly and unquestioningly. Quarrels lasted seconds and then were forgotten. Love conquers everything, but they were too young to channel this love into positive support for each other. Oh yes, this was indispensability. I was 'it' and had to stay that way.

Every three months, I went to one or the other of two specialists. They told me there were two in case one of them missed something the other might spot. The lady doctor would examine my back, feel under the arms and brush my boxer shorts with her hands. The male doctor would do the same, but push his fingers into my armpits until they hurt. He was always accompanied by a nurse. She remained with me behind the screen while I undressed. I asked why, but there was no answer. I sensed this was some modern paranoia and told the doctor that I trusted him. Thereafter the chaperone remained hovering in the background, but I was never allowed to be alone with him. I asked the lady doctor why she was never chaperoned and he was. As I suspected, it was fear of allegations which, it was assumed, would not be made against a woman. A couple of years went by and these examinations became a matter of routine. A couple of years after this and the chaperone was allowed to disappear.

'Just on my way to the c-a-n-c-e-r clinic,' I told one of the boys' teachers, spelling it out so that the children would not be concerned.

'That's nice,' came the reply.

That regular visit went as the others had with the exception that he looked between my toes.

'That's where they can hide,' he said. 'That's why we always look there.'

'But you haven't. I mean this is the first time you've looked there.'

He looked concerned, but it was not because I may have pointed out some oversight. Under my arm he had found a lump.

Uncle Charlie

Piers' godfather was Uncle Charlie. He was a tall, sporty stock-broker. I had known him since he was 19, more than two decades before. 'Watch a football match? I'd rather read the yellow pages' has always been a mantra of mine, so Charlie marked every one of my birthdays with a Newcastle United sup-porters' card.

'He lives in a new castle,' Piers proudly told his friends and, indeed, we visited him there. Although not a castle, he lived very comfortably with his wife, Sally, and children Freddy (a similar age to my boys) and James in a suburb of Newcastle. 'That day was the best' Charlie told me after our first family visit there in the glorious early autumn of 2007. Together we explored the beach at Howick where his parents had taken him as a boy, trod the ramparts at Berwick, ran round the Angel of the North at Gateshead and drove across the North Sea to Holy Island with the sat-nav telling us we were in the water. His boys and mine played together and we just enjoyed each other's company. All of us felt so close, so much part of a family.

Charlie's message to me the following July looked forward to his family's visit down south or ours to them in the north. I called to make the arrangements. His voice had changed.

'I've had this backache for a few months now – and a gippy tummy. Quacks don't know what it is. My son, Freddy, asked me, 'What age was your Daddy when he died, Daddy?' We laughed. He sounded like a 70 year old. He was 43.

A fortnight later, the backache was diagnosed as secondary bone cancer. The primary was angiosarcoma. It was terminal.

'Is Uncle Charlie going to die, Daddy?' Piers' eyes were enquiring; his voice trembled.

'Yes, I gather so, but no one can say when.'

'You told us cancer travels, Daddy.'

'Yes, it can and it did with Uncle Charlie. It travelled to his bones.'

'But your cancer was on your back and now your operation's under your arm. Has it travelled?'

'It may have, darling. That's what the operation's about.'

Ian turned round from where he had been eating. 'If you die, Daddy, who's going to look after us?'

Forever young

'How old are you, Daddy?'

'94.' The answer came as a knee-jerk. None of their business, so I'll just give them a number. Never got an answer from my parents when I was their age. Never had the temerity to ask. Better to err on the side of caution. Give them something far more than the real thing, they'll realise it's a spoof, get the message that I'm not telling them and it'll keep them quiet. When they find out, they'll be relieved rather than disappointed. It'll be like Father Christmas. They know I know, I know they know, they know I know they know. How wrong I was. They still believed in Father Christmas and believed me. This misinformation would be challenged daily.

'You were alive when Queen Victoria was on the throne.'

'Just missed her.'

'You're even older then the Queen. You don't look older than the Queen. How can you be so old? '

'Wearing well, boys.'

I kept it up for several years.

'How old was your dad when he died? You're almost as old as him. When I see his photos he looks much older than you.'

'Be he, indeed. Thanks, Ian, you pay me nice compliments.'

Piers was playing with his fingers. 'But your dad died when we were two and now we're seven, so how can you be 96 when he died at 94?'

'Ah, the mysteries of life, Piers.'

'H's mum says you'll get a telegram from the Queen in a few years when you're 100. What's a telegram?'

My 95th birthday came round, then my 96th.

'Dad, they told me at school that you're not 96, but I told them you told me you were. They tell me I'm lying.'

Time to come clean. In fact, 60 something or 90 something made little difference. My boys proudly told anyone who would listen that their dad was 63.

'Dad, they tell me you're not 63. They tell me I'm lying. They tell me you're 43.'

But it enabled me to play the age card.

'You don't have to do a penalty shoot-out with me. It's a hard job for a 63 year old. If you do, I can pick up the ball for you. You don't have to bend down, old chap.' Lars put a comforting hand on my arm.

'Oh, Daddy,' Ian sighed, wistfully. 'Nearly everyone's 60 these days.'

'I never knew you were so old!' the lady in charge of the boys' swimming school yelled up into the viewers' gallery. 'I read it in 'Fabulous'.' I yelled back down to her, apologising for disappointing her. What could I say?

A mum I met at the hairdresser was talking about her new husband-to-be and the problems people of 'our age' have in confronting prejudice. 'You must be my age,' she said. 'Early 40s.' When I told her my age, her hand went straight to her mouth. 'Fuck me,' she gasped. 'You look 20 years younger. My mother's 65.' The passing hair stylist gave a slight shriek. 'I haven't got leprosy, you know.' 'My girls will be so shocked,' she said – and on reflection added 'It'll give them hope for when they're old, too.'

I didn't look old; I didn't feel old; didn't smoke; hardly drank; led an active life; wasn't overweight. But I had lived a long time and that can't be done without getting old. Longevity seemed to be in the family. My father had lived until he was 94. Had it not been for his brain damage, he might well have made the century. My mother died when she was 87, but this was because of a hospital mistake. On the other hand, my best friends had died in their 20s. I just went on and on while other people disintegrated around me. It was not a conscious thought, but just a factor in my life. I assumed I would die sometime, but could not imagine how.

This was how I had felt when I made the decision back in 1999 to have children. I assumed I would be my father's age and just slip away quietly while my child would be in his or her early 40s and no longer at all dependent. The likelihood of an early demise was sufficiently unreal enough to enable me to make arrangements that were idealistic in the extreme. There was the house; there was an insurance policy; there were godparents. It seemed straightforward. It all hinged on the fact, as I saw it, that I was immortal – at least until I didn't need to be.

How wrong I was.

'Golden lads and girls all must, as chimney sweepers, come to dust.'

The bright side

'But it's such an incredible coincidence!' Charlie on the phone was animated.

'What is?'

'That we both have cancer!' He was positively brimming.

That I could think of more agreeable coincidences went unremarked. Any enthusiasm in a man in his condition was to be prized.

'Right now I've got an enlarged stomach and legs. It's water retention. I'm sort of the same straight down from my trunk to my feet. And you should see my penis.'

I sensed he wanted me to describe my own condition. Apart from an operation wound under my right arm, there was nothing to see. I was as I had always been. I struggled briefly to continue the theme.

'Like full leg version of housemaid's knee?'

'That's it. And I have to say, Ian, that this is real bonding.'

'Yup. If we had a hospital room together we'd have a great time. I have far too many things to do to have the time to die; too much to live for. Just like you. I want us to know each other for years, for our boys to grow up as friends and for us to have many more wonderful weekends like the last one. I'm really proud to have you as my friend and it's great that I can say to you everything that normally gets said when one is dead.'

'When we're better…'

'Yes. When.'

Thinking the unthinkable

The horrendous possibility of leaving my children without a parent, however ersatz, loomed large. How could they stay together if I weren't there? What would be the practicalities of the care of orphaned triplets? The answer came shortly after my diagnosis in a telephone call from my friend, Emma, as I was leaving the clinic following a checkup.

'I've been thinking about you. About your health. You have many friends. I know. I've met some of them. And I'm sure they'd be only too willing to help out, but I want you to know something. I love your children. I see them as my surrogate grandchildren. If anything were to happen to you, I would love to have them live with me and for me to bring them up.'

These were the most generous and selfless words I had ever heard. I felt my legs weaken and I clutched the door frame for support. There was no need for thought.

'What can I say? They're so young, so precious, so vulnerable. There's no one in the whole world to whom I would rather entrust the wellbeing of my little ones than to you.'

'Your sons are vulnerable, precious, clever, resilient, and have had the perfect start to their lives. I just hope and pray that all this is irrelevant and unnecessary.'

But if it were, my boys would be secure and loved. Although life for a single parent is all about thinking of other people, from this point on, I would have to think about me. A brief encounter with a dodgy sandwich laid me low for a day during which the boys stayed in their pyjamas and everyone remained unfed. As I drifted in and out of awareness on the sofa, a new and entirely novel lawlessness swept over the household.

'I'm telling. Yes, I am. I'm telling on you.'

Without anyone to tell and in the absence of a natural pecking order, their own sense of justice had to prevail.

'You ruin my life. I hate you. I wish you'd just go away or that Dad would put you on eBay, but no one would want you.'

'I want to be an only child. I wish you'd died at birth. Better, yes better, I wish you hadn't been born.'

'I didn't ask to be born. You're horrible and selfish and Dad loves me best.'

The words swam in and out of my consciousness. By the time I was able to stand up, the children were back in harmony, playing together. Their tirades had brief lives. Whatever it was that lay under the skin, erupted instantly, the boil was lanced on the spot and quiescence returned until the next time which could be almost immediately. When we arrived at a friend's too early the following day, I realised that they had devised a *Lord of the Flies* way of working together that enabled them to turn my watch back an hour and keep quiet about it.

My one day's brush with illness had taught me that boys are

pack animals. They need a leader and, if that leader looks as if he's heading for the end of the road, they vie for the position themselves. There's no place for a leader who isn't leading. As an only child, I imagined I would have been sympathetic and helpful if for no other reason than I would be fearful of being left alone. The dynamics of triplicity ensured that sibling rivalry triumphed over all other emotions. Daddy's in charge and if he isn't playing the part and is just vomiting in the loo, he's super-numerary. Survival was essential or everything would come tumbling down.

11

Mortality

Life goes on

'Who will look after us if you die, Daddy?'

'Emma will.'

Question answered, the boys carried on with their home-work. Ian needed to do his 'Geography'. In fact, it was always General Knowledge – 'GK' – but it was all the same to him.

'I'm never going to get all my Geography done now 'cos the days are getting shorter.'

'Well as I'm the one who taps the words into Google and then you copy down the answers, I wouldn't say you have much of a job to do.'

Scanned, poked and prodded

'Melanoma's not well known.' The oncologist had his serious face on. 'It's likely to drain to the nearest lymph nodes. If the original melanoma is less than 1.5, it's unlikely to cause further problems. Yours was 3.9, so it was relatively thick. Now that it has migrated, the next step is to have PET scans. They will show if the melanoma has spread elsewhere.'

'And if it has?'

'Then we treat accordingly, although it's not really treatable by chemotherapy. About 10%. It's likely that your scans will be clear. Put it this way, the melanoma in the node I removed last week wouldn't show. It was about a centimetre. Generally infected nodes are the size of a golf ball.'

'And if it hasn't or doesn't seem to have spread?'

'Then we remove the remaining lymph nodes on that side. That's the nationally accepted procedure, although as with much of the treatment of melanoma, there are dissenting opinions. Having done this, it's likely that that the remaining nodes will be clear, but we can't tell unless they are removed. There is also a chance that you won't regain full mobility in your arm and that there will be permanent swelling.'

'But won't this take away part of my immune system? And if, as you said, the melanoma is likely to migrate to the nearest lymph nodes, where would it drain to if there weren't any there?'

My mobile vibrated. I excused myself and took it out of my pocket. It was Emma. I passed my phone to the doctor. He patiently went through all that he had told me.

'No, I'm not going to give a prognosis.' He looked into the middle distance. I imagined what he was being asked. 'No, I'm not going to give a worst-case-scenario. I've explained what's happening to Ian and he understands. If you want to ask me questions, I'll answer with both of you here in front of me, not over the phone.'

'He seems a very nice man.' I had regained my phone.

'Yes, but no one really knows about melanoma. I'm getting an informed viewpoint. There may be others. I really need a second opinion about these nodes. When they're gone they're gone and bang goes that part of my immune system.' Why, for instance, can't I hang onto them? He checks to see if there's a lump and, if there is, then I have the lot out.

The second opinion was quite straightforward. 'If they were my nodes, I'd have them out.'

With this opinion came the straightforward information that I knew would shape the way I viewed the rest of my life.

'You may be completely free of the disease. But you will never know this. Only if you die of something else at 90 or 100 will you know that you had been clear.'

Quite what shape this would take, I had no idea. My old school hymn book that had accompanied me every day from 11 until I was 18 contained a hymn that I had sung on many occasions. Even as a child, the words in one of the lines struck me as being worthy of debate: '... and live each day as if 'twere thy last.' On the one hand, I understood the exhortation that each day should be lived well and morally as there would be no time for undoing wrongs done if this were the last day. On the other hand, as a Sixth-Former, I was dealing with Sartre and Camus and the existentialist concept of living for the moment. One of the characters in 'Les Justes' says, while discussing the concept of ends justifying means as he carries out an assassination: 'Vivre pour le moment. C'est la seule raison d'être' – a philosophy I had observed the children tending towards whereby given a pair of scissors, a hot day and long trousers, they might well have created shorts without regard for the winter that would come. How should I live each day?

'So', I observed to the oncologist. 'I may be quite well.'

'Yes.'

'Or not.'

'Yes.'

Which did not get me further forward. Would I continue to be, or not? Would I continue to be able to do everything myself as I had done, or not? Always I had been able to rely on me. Now I was not so sure. The children had to be safeguarded. That was the priority, but should I assume that this would be with me or without me and to what extent should I change my life, and by extension theirs, to allow for my early death which might not happen? Already I could feel control slipping from me.

My friend would have the children. We were introducing them to her home in the New Forest. We had looked at possible schools there. Very soon too, after the operation for the removal of the remaining nodes, I would lose my ability to drive for a month, a freedom that I had enjoyed since six in the morning of my 17th birthday. I had taken on a young man to drive for us. P. might even have to help me to dress. What would it be like, being dependent? I had been the strong one, the one people depended on, the one who made the decisions and took charge. The one who went it alone and had children. Out went these brainsickly thoughts. Life had begun again at 52. I wasn't about to give it up so soon.

The final visit

I had never seen the point in texting until Uncle Charlie started sending me messages to my mobile phone. 'It was lying there in hospital in the dark that did it for me,' he said. 'There was always noise – people hacking and spitting, crying and groaning. I couldn't sleep. And there was my little bit of civilisation with blue lights glowing softly. So I pushed the buttons and there was a new world of contact. It was gr8.' When he learned about my condition, the texts became more intimate. He told me about the water retention, his swollen penis, his bulging scrotum. He used expletives that I had never known him to use before. It was his way of telling me what was happening and how he was feeling – all at one remove. All sanitised through technology. I wanted to see how he was, how this disease could be. Was I being so selfish in wanting to see him, hug him, tell him I was there? I phoned. 'I can be there tomorrow. The boys are with Auntie Claire for the weekend. They're seeing the fireworks at Legoland. Just say if you'd like me to come.'

He was as fed up as could be, bloated and all but immobile. He agreed immediately and I flew to Newcastle.

The frozen north

'And I find myself saying, 'I really don't want your beef casserole.' It sounds dreadful, but we could be inundated with people wanting to help. My parents are two miles down the road; Charles's mum is a few hundred yards away and there are his sisters and, well, all our family is in Newcastle.' Sally, Uncle Charlie's wife, talked brightly as she set about making lunch.

'Don't knock it, Sally. You don't know when you're well off. Wish I had a relative to say 'no' to.'

Charlie was gaunt from the waist up and bloated from the waist down. 'It's so hard to breathe. I say to them can't you just let me stand up and put a couple of taps onto my feet and drain it all away. I just get so puffed out, as though my lungs just can't get enough air into them, but, no, they say they can't do this and my body will just have to get rid of the fluid itself. It used to be good. I could go out for walks, but now...' His voice trailed away. Both hands moved towards his feet dismissively. 'Now, I just don't know. If it's going to carry on being like this...'

'But you have to believe the doctors. I guess they must have seen swelling like this before and know it'll go away. You have to believe them.'

His two small sons greeted me wide-eyed and smiling. 'Thank you very much,' they chorused and off they went with their presents. Sally went back to the kitchen. I sat alone with Charlie. He unbuttoned his shirt and took off his slippers.

'I dunno, it's just all this. Look at my belly; look at these piggy toes… When I'm better, we'll do it again – the beach and Holy Island.'

'Of course we will, but, Charlie, if anything happens to you, please let me carry on seeing your boys. Without you, they'd be, well, surrounded by women. No man in their lives. Put me into your letter of wishes. That would make it special.'

It may have been presumptuous to say this, may have introduced a touch of grim reality into a cosy family Sunday afternoon.

Charlie needed to sleep. He had arranged for his mum to look after me for a couple of hours and I drove my rental car down the road to her house. She stood in the rain, hands by her side, a faint smile of recognition. We drove off in silence.

'He won't see Christmas, you know.'

I indicated left and pulled into the side of the road.

'You've been playing the game, haven't you? It's terminal. This swelling, it's another step in the illness. He's an incredibly brave man, but it's all a game. I think I play it myself sometimes, too. It's just awful. I have friends who are doctors. They've told me. Well maybe Christmas – if he's lucky. He's a goner. It breaks my heart.'

'I don't know what to do with this. He's positive, upbeat. We're talking about when he's better.'

She changed the subject and asked about my situation.

'Well, of course, I'm going to go on and on.'

'Aha. Just like Charles isn't going to die.'

In the grim November rain and cold, we retraced in the dark what my family and I had last seen in the summer sunshine of our family weekend the previous year. With lights blazing, the Sage Centre was a schooner with all its sails set. The city lights twinkled; the winking bridge winked. My heart froze.

*

Not saying goodbye

'Next visit, I'll bring the car.' I sat in the rented Fiesta trying to get my portable sat-nav to stick to the dashboard with blutak. 'Should be during the Christmas hols when I can drive again. It's OK. Don't stand there. I need to fiddle with my sat nav.' I could hardly see it through the mist in front of my eyes. Charlie waved and closed the door. Six weeks later, without his realising what was happening, a chest infection took hold and he died. By another coincidence, I, too, had a chest infection and was too ill to travel to his funeral service. Some weeks later, after an x-ray, I was told that I had had double pneumonia. 'I thought it was a bad cold with a bit of a cough.' There are none so smug as those who have walked round with double pneumonia.

'Does he take sugar?'

'I feel sticky. There's a trickle.' A bottle wrapped in towelling hung from my belt. From my armpit where the lymph nodes had been a few days before, a tube led into a bottle which swung heavily around my knees. The boys were cautious, solicitous. They kept their distance, kissing my hand, touching my outstretched arm, aware that the bottle which they had asked to inspect contained something that was essentially Daddy and needed to be left alone.

When the boys were safely tucked in, I stood in my bedroom, arms dangling, feeling damp and immobile. P. unbuttoned my shirt and peeled it away from my body.

'I'll get you to the hospital.'

'I've asked your carer to get you undressed.' The nurse was matter-of-fact and efficient; her voice perhaps a touch louder than before. She had made an assumption about who P. was that crystallised his changed role and what I had become. She showed him how to clean the wound and change my dressings. Her conversation was to him. 'How long ago did he have the procedure? How has he been since? How do you think the drain may have become detached? You'll need to take his temperature.' Had my arm not been over my head, I would have waved to tell her that I was actually there and had not lost the power of speech or rational thought. Had she been able to offer tea, no doubt she would have asked P. if I took sugar.

Back at home, he gently let the sponge touch my skin as the water from the shower trickled over me, patted me dry, peeled away the gauze and applied a fresh square. I was an invalid. I had been bathed for the first time since I was five. I could not have wished for a kinder, more sensitive carer, but there I was – utterly dependent and tasting life as a patient.

'Thank you.'

I rubbed wetness from the corner of my eye. He squeezed my hand.

Coming clean

'Maybe you could see if there are any drugs trials available?' I told Emma I would explore the possibility. I couldn't imagine what Charlie's sons' lives were like without their dad. For mine, their plight would be even worse. Orphaned as seven year olds. It was unthinkable. I just had to stay alive. A few weeks later, I started a trial of Avast-M, the 'M' being for Melanoma, under the aegis of Professor Dr O. in Southampton.

Dr O. was very bouncy. That was not only because of his shape. 'You vill come every three veeks at ze beginning. The trial involves computer randomisation. 50% vill get the treatment; 50% vill not. Vhether you are lucky to get it or not get it is eqvivocal. It may be that it does good; it may be that it does nothing at all. There may be side-effects. Ve vill give you a CT scan and an x-ray. Ve vill look at your bloods und zen ve start.' His eyes twinkled. Over the years, his twinkle and his shape intensified. How he managed this when surrounded by death and tragedy, I have no idea. 'Ah, Dr O,' I would say at every visit, 'I see you remain undiminished.' He chuckled and we swapped stories about our sons.

Three weeks later, I returned. I was among the 50% to receive the drug. Whether I had drawn the short or long straw, I had no idea. Certainly there was no question of the undrawn 50% having a placebo. The first infusion of the treatment via a cannula took an hour and a half. 'Can't you just shove it in? I've got to pick the children up from school.' The Chinese doctor, S, was reassuring. 'It won't always take this long. We want to see that you are OK with this treatment, so we take it slowly. Next time, it will only take an hour.' The clear liquid drained drip by drip into my system. I felt fine. A follow-up questionnaire was to elicit whether I noticed any changes to my way of life. I was happy to answer all the questions positively. 'No', I did not have to take naps. Chance would be a fine thing. 'No', incredibly with three active sons, I did not get headaches. 'How are you?' now, for a change, assumed immense proportions. 'OK.' 'Just OK?' 'No, fine.' 'Does that mean really well?' It was as well as I could muster after a 4.30 am awakening from a small boy who had just had a bad dream. 'Your blood pressure is elevated.' 'After a 40 mile drive, surrounded by medical machinery, obliged to focus on my being and with a hammer drill blasting into the floor above, I wonder why?' 'You're not very well endowed.' 'Sorry about that.' 'No, I meant, your veins aren't prominent. Let's try the other arm.' 'Two band-aids. Do I get a sticker for bravery to impress the boys?' None was forthcoming. I would have to show them the plasters.

'Any lumps, bumps, or anything unusual?'

'I don't think so, but I really don't know what I should be looking for.'

The examinations in the hospital drugs trial were different. I was touched gently on the neck, on the stomach and under the arms. After the surgeon in Basingstoke had had a go at me, I knew I had been touched. I was just the punter, but I wondered how they would find anything that needed to be found after such a mild poke. 'Maybe J. could take a look?' 'Oh, we can do this.' 'How I put this correctly? You're women. I'd prefer a man to examine me.' They looked surprised. 'OK. I'll come clean. I'm used to being hurt during these pokings and I think J. can poke about without bothering whether he hurts or not on the basis that I guess he has the sensitivity of a lavatory seat.' 'That hurt enough for you?' became an accompaniment to J's examinations. 'Yes, thanks. I know you've been there. But you've never looked at my feet.'

For the 19 sessions of the drugs trial, I drove to Southampton every third Friday and had needles stuck into me, blood sucked out and jollop drained in. I saw people whose melanoma had not been diagnosed as early as mine had been who would have given anything to have had the chance of Avast-M; saw those with other conditions; realised how lucky I was.

'How did it go from there to there, Daddy?' Ian traced a line from my shoulder blade to my underarm. 'That's where your angel's wing would be.'

'No one really knows, but maybe in the blood.'

'But,' said Piers, drawing knowledge from his science lessons, 'Blood travels everywhere.'

'Nastiness trends to end up in the lymph.'

'But you haven't got any on that side, Daddy. If it can't stop there, where does it go?'

'That's a question. Maybe the other lymph.'

Three pairs of eyes travelled from one underarm to the other. Lars's went straight across. Piers' and Ian's went down the body and up.

'So does it stop somewhere while it's going there?'

'Maybe, Ian, we hope not, but it may not go down and then up. It may not go straight across. The doctor tells me it may go to the large organ nearest to the original melanoma.' I tapped my head.

'The brain?' Piers said, knowingly.

'What does the lymph do?' Lars asked.

'It deals with, let me put it this way, 'unpleasantness' and helps the body recover. If something happens to this arm, the lymph tries to make it better.'

'But you haven't got lymph there.' Ian was concerned.

'This is why Daddy has to be careful. If he gets stung or scratched by a thorn, the arm can't deal with the infection and may stay damaged. If there's swelling, it may not go down.'

'I don't want you to die, Daddy.' Ian stroked my arm and pressed his body against mine.

'I'll do my best not to, Ian.'

Had I done the right thing in being so upfront? That's the problem with being on one's own. There's no constant adult presence to bounce ideas around with. One of the boys' former teachers pulled no punches.

'They know that Daddy has had cancer. I told them.'

'I'm very doubtful about children being given information they can't do anything with.'

'I think they need to know the truth, how things are, what might happen.'

'And then have something to worry about for no good reason? No. They needed to be told when there was a need to tell them, not at such an early stage. If something happens that changes their life, they need to know what's being done about this change and how it will be made right for them, not be given some abstract possibility that just complicates their lives.'

'I really think it all depends on how the whole situation is handled. It's like dealing with porn on the internet. When they stumbled across fellatio, we all had a good laugh about it and talked about the strange people who liked that sort of thing. The same with addictions, bad language and all the other horrors of grown-up life. They're going to know that there are bad things around. There's no point in pretending they don't exist. They can be talked about and disapproved of. My friend, Emma, had the boys stay with her while I was in hospital and she taught them all the rude words. I say 'taught them', but they'd heard them already. She thought she'd get it all over and done with in one go. They came back full of 'see you next Tuesday'. Rather her than me, though', I admitted.

'See you next Tuesday?'

'Yes. Think about it.'

How refreshing to get another opinion. That, I decided, was a huge advantage of having a partner and a real disadvantage for me. I would have to do my best to consider a counter argument to all my child-rearing ideas. On second thought, that's the way madness lies. I decided that carrying on confident about my own rectitude was preferable to being in the state of constant indecision that was the alternative I saw.

12

Fury

Tantrooms and flying fists

'I don't do fury,' I told one of the mums. She had been telling me about how she used hers to effect with her son.

'Don't or can't?' she enquired.

'Never have,' was my response.

Can't might have been more honest, but it needed some thought. At that point, fury was a passion that I had not indulged myself in and an indulgence it would be. The loss of control that is implicit in the emotion is something I was quite unused to. 'Rather cross' I could do and had done, but being out of control of myself was unthinkable. Careful, guarded, wary was what I had been right from the moment of my father's brain damage when I was eight. I knew that I had to be careful, had to watch my step.

With this approach, starting a business at 21 when most people are young and carefree was not a problem. I was already going on 40. I would take the Lady Macbeth approach and try to see the future in the instant before doing anything. If I were to do X, then the result would be Y, or Z, or any combination of these, or something different. By the time I had worked out potential ramifications, any passion would have evaporated.

With the children, I would reflect on possible consequences to my actions so that my reaction would be studied and measured, not because I thought such a response preferable, but because I could not respond in any other way.

When little Ian was biting his baby brothers, the district nurse had told me to bite him back. By the time I had thought what might happen, had peeled back his sleeve and opened my mouth for the gentle touch of teeth on skin that was to come, he was ready, teeth bared, and had drawn blood from my hand. When the time came for them to exchange punches, I was only too aware that any of that from me would destroy my argument that civilised people didn't hit. As I saw it, a blow from me would have ended the immediate incident and stored up destroyed credibility for the future. Besides, a man telling a child what he could do with a punch — and the words 'middle of next week' were used — was, I thought, a powerful lesson in self-control and that, just because you can do it, doesn't mean that you should do it. Nevertheless, I sometimes felt my fist twitch. The self-control was becoming difficult.

'You hit my daddy!' Lars would scream, hurling himself into me, burying his tears in my chest while Ian took out his frustration in punches to whatever parts of my body remained accessible.

'Let this teach you,' I would say when the heat of the moment had passed and I showed them the redness, 'that although I could hit out and, yes, it would stop you, I didn't because hitting is wrong and I won't do exactly what I tell you not to do, no matter how much I'm provoked.'

The conclusion was invariably a tearful 'sorry, Daddy' and, on my part, a relieved thankfulness that I had not succumbed to fury — wherever that may have led. I suspect that the brothers saw it as weakness. For me, it was a strength and yet another side to being a parent whereby one cannot do as one wishes and has to put oneself last.

At the same time as I was considering the notion of fury, passion and powerful emotion, I could see that I was also providing a rationale for why I had chosen to be in this single parent situation. I just had not felt sufficiently passionate about anyone to wish to marry them. Or maybe I had felt cautious about letting myself go. It was too easy to trace it all back to my father's brain damage and I certainly had no wish to perceive myself as a victim. I had and gave unconditional love and that was enough. Or so I thought. I was beginning to discover that sweet reason was one thing. Real life was another.

Stage fright

'Loser!'

Ian had been late finishing brushing his teeth and I had read the first two sentences of that bedtime's story. My second son, like a domestic cat gone feral, was spitting venom and toothpaste in my direction, shrieking in rage, 'You're old and I hate you!'

'OK, Ian, yes I am and I'm sure you do, but you'll get over it.'

The response was a punch in the stomach. I keeled over. Breath regained, I said in a calm voice, 'Now get over your tantrum, Ian, and sit on the step outside the door.'

A succession of blows followed. I raised my hand and immediately lowered it. Occupying the moral high ground was not going to be easy, but that's where I thought I always needed to be. Even at eight, he was still small enough to lift along the corridor, but he was certainly not minded to sit on the step. I knew what I would try. A 21st-century solution came to my mind as a way of dealing with this age-old problem. I would film him. I went to get my camera. Ian grabbed my leg, punching where it would hurt and felling me once more.

'Look, Ian, everyone sees you as a cute little boy, but your brothers and I know that you can be really nasty. I think it's about time everyone knew what you were really like.' Was this good parenting? What long-term repercussions might there be? I imagined that he saw me as weak. Is that what his brothers thought, too? Lars was shocked and crying at this sudden deterioration of the bedroom into a screaming war zone. Piers had put his head under the duvet right at the start of hostilities. They shouldn't be seeing this. They needed to know that I could see Ian off on my own terms. Up again, I shook Ian off my leg and opened the sideboard door where my camera lay. On the glass top stood a china cat and mouse that had been Ian's favourites. He picked up the cat and made as if to hurl it against the wall. Taking advantage of his temporary distraction, I grabbed the camera, pulled it from its case and pushed the button.

Ian smiled at the lens.

'Now tell the camera what you've been doing.'

Ian smiled warmly and whispered, 'No.'

Lars seized his chance. 'Well, I'll tell the camera. He's been horrible and hit Daddy.'

I turned the camera off. Ian rushed at Lars and floored him. The camera case went flying into my face. I switched on. Peace descended in an instant. So did silence. As long as the camera was on, the only words from Ian were, 'Don't believe him. This is Loser Films Incorporated.'

His brothers in bed, Ian came with me to watch my regular chores of emptying the dishwasher and folding the laundry, everything done while clutching the camera.

'If you're not proud of what you do, don't do it.'

'Sorreeeee.'

A tearful Ian clutched my hand and went to bed, leaving me

to assess what had happened. Children can explode. Maybe I should be grateful for having two who did not. I had no qualifications for dealing with anger management for that is what I assumed it was. Or were there causes deeper than having been thwarted that underlay his outburst? I decided years before that I would not over-analyse the actions of a child. Children are childish – and volatile and unpredictable and want immediate gratification.

'When are you going to delete the films?'

'When there's no longer any need to keep them.'

'Who're you going to show them to?'

'No one at the moment, so that's as good as having them deleted, isn't it?'

Ian was not convinced. Nor was I. When I was a boy, a parent would have lashed out before anything developed and the child would have been stilled by a mixture of fear and respect. I was left unsure whether my son felt either for me. The outpouring of grief at the end told me there was love, plenty of it, probably tinged with guilt. Nevertheless, I was sure that he had seen my physical inaction as inability rather than disinclination.

Battle lines

'You used to admire Lars.'

'He's dirty. He doesn't brush his teeth for two minutes and I saw him wash his hands without using soap.'

A few days later, we were preparing to go to 'Camp' during the half-term holiday. Lars and Piers put small toys in their pockets.

'You can't take them!' Ian shrieked suddenly, his face reddening and his fists clenching. 'Daddy, they can't take them. They'll lose them and I'll worry all day that they'll lose them and then we'll have to spend a lot of time looking for them. They can't take them!'

'So you'll rush up to them and hit them and I'll pull you off and you'll hit me? All for what? A couple of toys? So what if they lose them? They're their toys, not yours. Does it really matter?'

Although his brothers defused the situation by not taking their toys, the peace was short-lived. That evening, Piers took a large tub of building bricks out of the cupboard and started to open them on the floor. A nuclear missile with accurate trajectory, Ian launched himself across the room and slammed the half-open lid onto his hand. Piers squealed in pain and burst into tears. Lars leapt to his defence.

'Whad'ya do that for? We're building a set for our film.'

Ian's fist shot out, catching Lars on the side of the head. 'You'll make a mess. I'll have to clear it up!'

I scooped Lars into my arms. Piers fled. There was a sudden crack and sting across my back, then the side of my face. Ian had pulled the belt out of his trousers. He lunged for Lars. For the first time ever, the red mist rose and I pinned Ian to the bed, hands spread, arms flailing. Contact was made.

'Don't you ever think that I'll stand by and do nothing, Ian.' I was trembling at the enormity of it. Ian was ashen-faced and in tears. Lars screamed into my arms. In the space of just a few minutes, a calm domestic scene had been transformed into a battlefield, but the lines had been re-drawn. Ian had seen my peacemaking as inaction; sweet reason as weakness. How would this be seen?

'Sorreeeee, Daddy.'

'Are you going to hit Daddy again?'

Ian shook his head. Tears sprinkled out at either side.

'Can you film 'Beowulf and Grendel', Daddy? It's by www.paperproductions.co.uk, it is.' In a few seconds, it was, for his brothers, as though nothing had happened. The events of a day were mine of a week. In their compressed time-scale one experience followed another without pause for reflection and it was that flow that was propelling me.

'Tell the camera who they are, Lars.'

'They're Grendel and Beowulf.' Lars pointed to small pieces of torn paper with humanoid outlines drawn on them in pencil, one bearing a 'G' on its front, the other a 'B'. Smaller pieces had been torn to represent Hrothgar's thanes. 'This,' his finger moved to a small strip 'is the table and this', he folded a sheet of A4, 'is Heorot, the mead hall. Bowulf is going to tear Grendel's arm off. I can't do it now because… well, it has to be done later when you're filming.'

Lars stood up in his maroon striped pyjamas and faced the camera. 'This is Grendel and Beowulf by Lars's www.paperproductions.co.uk and this,' he beckoned Piers to appear from behind a chair, 'is my assistant, Piers.' Piers showed the camera a small banner with 'www.paperproductions.co.uk' in joined-up handwriting. 'Here is the story…'

Ian watched out of the camera's range, stroking one of the cats. Later, when I had given them their hugs and kisses in bed, I looked for the domain name on Easyspace, found it was available, bought it and created the bones of a web site for them. I transferred Lars's film from my camera onto a CD and deleted the footage of Ian. I put the cats' baskets in the kitchen and went to bed.

The professional perspective

'It's OK to be angry.'

The words, simple in themselves, were a revelation. The lady at the school who saw children privately about their emotional problems was placatory.

'I would never have hit my parents. It was just unthinkable. And I've never sat down and had a chat with any parent whose child has hit them. People don't talk about this. It's like admitting domestic violence. I assumed he had crossed a boundary that could never be uncrossed.'

'But this is the sign of a free child. A child who is able to express himself.'

'I never was. I knew that I had to look over my shoulder. I could never let go.'

'But what Ian has to do is express his anger acceptably.'

'He's told me he wants a cushion.'

'There you are. He knows exactly what he needs.'

The power of charm

'I love you, Daddy. I'm sorry for hitting you. I don't want you to die. It's all my fault. I'm sorry for my assessment grades. I wish I'd been the fourth embryo. The one that died.'

'Look, Ian, Daddy has no plans to die any time soon and whatever's wrong with him – and it may be that nothing's wrong – is not your fault, but it makes Daddy sad when you're unhappy.' It had become second nature to refer to myself in the third person. I was speaking as Daddy with all the responsibilities that job entailed rather than as a human being with a first name.

Daddy was reasonable, self-effacing, even-handed and judicious. Indeed, Daddy-mode had been switched-on for so long, following on from the Carer-mode that had lasted even longer, that Daddy had quite forgotten who he really was. I briefly toyed with the idea that I was, maybe, not so different from my challenging middle son. 'I just want you to be happy.' I could not issue the standard exhortation that I wanted him only to try his best as what his assessment card revealed possibly was his best. For an eight year old's progress to be minutely quantified as to effort and achievement in 13 subjects was not what I could remember from my school days and, while it felt good to see high grades and class positions, they mattered surprisingly little to me. I was ambitious for them only insofar as they felt content to be themselves. If this coincided with academic success, so much the better, but it was not a sufficient end in itself.

The happiness that comes from fulfilment is the best feeling and that is all I wanted for my sons. I remembered how I strove for success to please an implacable parent and, in the distant days before children, assumed that I would expect this from any offspring I might have. The reality of parenthood had changed my expectations out of recognition. Measurable standards were what the school system dealt in, though. A wise lady had told my boys and me 'It's charm that will get you everywhere. It doesn't matter how thick you are. No one will notice if you're charming.' But charm, like honesty, decency and love could not be weighed in the balance. If you didn't know your six times table by the time you were eight, this was a failing. Ian had just reached his four times and was found wanting. No matter that he would 'get there' eventually; he had not got there yet and his other character qualities did not compensate for this fundamental failing. This he knew and accepted and it hurt. Here was a bright eight year old who knew what the world regarded as success and, if he did not achieve this, he had failed.

'I'm no good. I can't do anything.'

'Just enjoy school, Ian. That's all you need to do. Enjoy it and it will all come to you.'

'Mr P. was teaching us adverbs this morning. He said 'the boy ran down the street' and asked us to say how. I put my hand up and said 'fearlessly.' Mr P. told me to stand on my chair. He played some special music and put a crown on my head and told me I'd become the first king for the day. When he said this, one of the girls said 'booo!'. So he got a song called 'Funeral Music', took B's long metal ruler and chopped her head off.'

'Mr D. took us for football and said to Ian 'You're so hopeless I'm going to get someone else to take your place – a first year girl.' Everyone laughed and Ian went red.'

'Yes, Daddy, and then he said to him that his granny could play better than Piers and she's been dead for 10 years.'

'And, Dad, then he said that we should practise power kicking. He put the ball down and said 'If I wanted to kick Piers' head off, I wouldn't do it like this 'cos I wouldn't shift it off his body. I'd do it like this.' And he put his foot a special way and said, 'that's Piers' head in the trees and Lars and Ian are shouting for joy.' And then we scored and he went 'toot toot' with his whistle.'

'Oh, Daddy, we had science with Mr G. today. He asked how long it took for the earth to go round the sun and only B. put his hand up and gave the answer. He asked five more questions and only B. put his hand up, so Mr G. said 'OK, B. you're the teacher now – and he went out.'

13

Changes

Working your audience

'Dear Mr Muckles' read the letter that arrived through the post one morning. 'Thank you for the lovely holiday and the lovely things we did like Supercamp and Scotland and everything else. I am having lots of fun, but chapel is rather boring. I do miss you sometimes. I have lots of friends and always play games. I have invented a game about shooting. I have got lots of credits and no debits. I am having buckets of fun with Mr B. In English we are reading Narnia and we are having lots of cool matches, but I don't really like games. Love from Piers.'

'And we have a competition when we've done our work. We have to push Potty down Everest. We start at base camp and answer some questions then we climb up bit by bit and if we can make it to the top, we can send him flying. We get tuck, too.'

As I discovered when I scooped the damp wrappers out of the washing machine, tuck was a constant motivating factor along with credits, performance awards and certificates. The more rewards the child received, the more points the child's House scored. There were debits for failure and these took away from the points all the children in the House had worked for. They were published each week on the notice-board. So in the microcosm of life that was the school I had chosen for them, they worked for treats and either gained peer group approval for the points they earned or disapproval for those they lost. All this surrounded by teachers, most of whom were fabulously charismatic to the point of unemployability anywhere else, who captivated their young charges with their enthusiasm and the unpredictability of their delivery.

'Now who was the bored young man?' The class had put on a tableau of Renoir's *Les Parapluies* in front of the school at that morning's chapel service with all the children taking parts in the crowd and dressing accordingly. The Headmaster was about to give out his notices and had stepped to the front of the stage. Piers raised a shy hand. 'Step forward, young man. Aha. I like this.' A hand flicked out and removed the cloth cap from Piers' head. 'I'll wear it, if you don't mind. Now if I get boring while I read out these notices, let me know.' Piers flushed red and looked at his shoes. On went the announcements of who had done well in which match and where the next fixtures were to be played. There was a roar of laughter from children and parents. Piers' shoulders had slumped and his head had fallen to one side. His face remained deadpan. 'Young man, you have stolen your Headmaster's show. Come to the study afterwards for tuck.'

The boys' school was set in a hundred acres of countryside, woodland and formal gardens. These were lovingly tended by staff, many of whom had known no other work. 'They're surrounded by loveliness,' I told one of the mums. She assumed I was being cynical. In fact, it was intended as an observation on their condition. Whatever the season, there was beauty surrounding them and excellent teachers to encourage their awareness and appreciation of this. 'We must never take anything for granted,' said one of their friends in an assembly Piers' class

gave in Chapel one morning. The speaker's face remained
downcast, glum. The next speaker remarked on the joys of
nature in a similar deadpan way. 'Then look around and enjoy
it!' my inner voice was shrieking. I hoped they were subdued
because they assumed this was what was expected in a religious
service, in an environment, Piers had told me, where everyone
was a serious believer and they were all contemplating their seri-
ousness.

In an encouragement to consider beauty, the congregation
was invited to look at blown-up pictures of everyday objects
and guess what these beautiful crystalline shapes were. 'Tip of
a ballpoint pen!' 'Fly's eye!' Their expansive and genial
Headmaster, trained in his craft as a holiday entertainer, took up
the theme in his address. 'When I was very young', he said, 'My
family lived near the sea. And what did the incoming waves do?
They went 'whoosh-swiiish! What sound did they make?' The
children responded in kind. 'And when they went back, they
pushed the sand back and the sand went 'rrrrrrrr'. What sound
did the sand make? And so all night there was a (pause while the
children added the effect) and (another pause for the other
effect). So with all this (pause) and (pause) when we had visitors, they would come down in the morning and say 'couldn't
get a wink of sleep', but, you know, I never heard anything. For
me there was silence all night.' His young audience was mes-
merised, his point made.

'I so enjoyed your assembly,' I told the children when I collected them that evening.

'Harry got a debit today because someone pushed him out
of a window.'

'You're really lucky to go to such a wonderful school, you
know. Your Head was on top form. He had everyone eating out
of his hand. An object lesson in how to hold an audience.'

'It was Charles who made him do it. To get some tuck. It

wasn't fair that he got a debit. He cried.'

As far as the eye could see, skeletal trees were silhouetted by a pale winter sun shining out of a blue-grey sky, tinged pink.

'Isn't this beautiful boys?'

'What's for dinner, Dad?'

One on one on one on one

I suddenly realised one day over Christmas when they were eight that I hadn't spoken to Piers on his own for three years, at least not completely on his own with a brother nowhere near. A dear friend we were staying with suggested that I take out each of them for the day while she looked after the remaining two.

'Isn't this great, Piers?' I said to the small boy on the monorail at Beaulieu, high above the grounds at the end of December with a biting easterly wind carrying shards of rain into the pod. He nodded his agreement and hunched back into his school waterproof, teeth chattering.

'But you didn't get me what I wanted for Christmas, Daddy.'

'What was that?'

'Ian and Lars's heads on a plate.'

When Lars's turn came, he was in no doubt where he wanted to go.

'Beaulieu please, Dad.'

Fortunately the monorail was closed as ice had coated the steel access stairs to the little station. We tried the 'Top Gear' tent. It was unheated. We were the only customers.

'I don't really mind having brothers. But I only love you, Dad.'

Ian's passion was for birds of prey, so when his turn came, I assumed it would be a trip to the nearby bird sanctuary. By now snow was forecast and I doubted that the birds would be on their best form.

'Where to, Ian?'

'Beaulieu, Daddy.'

The staff there greeted us like old friends and Ian even found some birds of prey, albeit stuffed, in the Palace.

'That was the Victorians' idea of conservation, Ian.'

'Couldn't you just sell them, Daddy? My brothers. I want to be an only child and stay with you.'

'But then you'd miss your friends at school, wouldn't you?'

His face dropped. He shook his head.

A concatenation of damned-back feelings poured out.

'They call me 'smalley'. They say I'm too little. That I'm a freak and a weirdo. And there's something else.'

'They're just having fun at your expense, Ian. They don't mean anything by it.'

'But I *am* small. And the older boys lift me up. And hang me,' he paused and looked down. 'Over the uri... urin... urination.'

'What!'

'In the changing room. After judo. And I didn't tell you, Daddy, because his brother's my friend and if he gets expelled, he'll have to leave, too. An older boy told him to stop. Both times. But he didn't. He held me by my ankles. Over the urination.'

It was 'Tom Brown's Schooldays' all over again.

'But not the third time. The older boy wasn't there then. I don't want to go there, Daddy.'

'Did he duck your head in the urinal?'

'What's that?'

'It's what you called the urination. Did your head go in?' I wondered what I was doing asking this question. What did it matter whether his head went in or not? Here was my little eight year-old being manhandled by an older child and all this while older children looked on.

'He just dangled me. He said I was so small and light that he could do it.'

How far should I take this without making it into a crisis? Inappropriate behaviour it certainly was, but was there anything more sinister? In a way I was relieved that someone else had been there, looking on, but should I simply accept that this was a traditional part of private school life, a rite of passage that meant nothing, or should I see it as assault? Boys will be boys, but preferably not suspended by their ankles. Should I laugh it off? A look at Ian's face told me I couldn't do that.

'Do you want me to tell the Head? You know I'll have to name names.'

'Yes, but don't get the names wrong, Daddy. It's the big one, not his brother. He's my friend. And I don't want him to leave. Waaah!'

But Ian's friend did not have to leave. Nor did his brother. There was an immediate investigation involving several of the teachers who spoke to Ian in a group as did the older boys involved. The result was communicated by e-mail that evening. It hadn't happened, or at least not in the way that Ian had said and, although he may have seen the urinal out of the corner of his eye, he wasn't dangled above it. The boy he had said did the dangling hadn't, but another boy whom Ian had not named had, but only in the area of the urinals and in any case Ian had enjoyed the ragging. As to the older boy, he could not have been there as he had to be somewhere else. It was all over.

Not for Ian, though. 'But they did do it, Daddy, and the boy I told you about was there.'

Some days later the boys were instructed to write letters of apology to Ian.

Ian was full of excitement when I collected him from school that evening. 'And W. said 'sorry for dangling you', so he was there, Daddy!'

'Let me see the letters, darling.'

'My teacher says I can't take them home.'

'But they are addressed to you, aren't they, Ian? I don't see why you can't have them.'

So what didn't happen may have happened, but the evidence was not to be given up. A grown-up in authority in front of any eight year-old could probably persuade him that the Archangel Gabriel was looking on and, while any adult is allowed to be represented by a friend at an enquiry, this facility is not accorded to a child at school. At least this parent was not invited to accompany his son. So 'Tom Brown' veered close to 'The Winslow Boy' and the older boy remained officially elsewhere. Every time a brother called another brother any rude name, it was other voices I heard.

'At private school, at least you get a better class of bully,' one of the parents remarked. 'It happens. You live with it.'

I was not so sure.

'I tell them to get on with it and that they'll meet unkind people everywhere,' I told a parent whose child had also been found wanting by the other eight year-olds.

'But then mine says 'Why should I, Mummy? Why should I have to put up with them and why are these people unkind?' and I just shrug my shoulders. I have no answer.'

'There's something else, Daddy. You know the photo of you that was in the S Room?' I remembered it well. The boys had taken me there a few months before. That room was a history of the school and was always open to visitors.

'Daddy,' the boys had said. 'Some girls came to us at lunch and said we were in the S Room in a newspaper there and they took us and showed us and it was the photo of us as babies that you have in the sitting room. And it said things about you. The girls asked us how much you were worth.'

There it was, open on a table, each page covered in plastic

film, a tabloid shock-horror story from years back that should have been in the next day's recycling, that should have no place in my children's school. It was an article that, to judge by the positive letters I received at the time, found no resonance with the great British public and led me to decide to offer my first book for publication. It left me wondering who could have placed it there and what they had wanted to achieve.

'Yes. It's not now. I mentioned it to the Head. Can't imagine why it was put there. Don't believe everything you read in the papers.'

'But it said things about you.'

'It said lots of silly things. Some papers weren't nice to Daddy when you were babies.'

'When the girls took us to see it, they asked how much you were worth. We said more than £600. We were right, Daddy, because each of us has £200 in his savings account, so we can give you that plus,' here Ian became animated. 'Plus, you've got what's in your wallet.'

14

The Internet

The facts of life

Piers was sitting on the stool in the bathroom that my parents had bought from Heals in the 1930s. He wriggled uncomfortably on its cork seat suspended over an art deco chrome frame. 'Dad.' He looked for a form of words and squirmed as his brain chose and discarded and chose again. 'Da-ad. I think I wee-ed out one of my sons today. It was a seed that came out in my wee at school. I know it. I saw it. It just came out. I couldn't stop it.'

He frowned, then brightened.

'How many seeds have I got?'

'Millions, Piers.'

'Oh, no, Dad. That means that I can have thousands of children, well hundreds. What am I going to do with them?'

'It all depends on the number of eggs they fertilise and there are far fewer eggs than there are seeds.'

'How many seeds did you use to make us, Daddy?'

'Just three out of millions.'

'They must be very small.'

Was getting ready for school in under 10 minutes the right time to discuss the circumstances of their conception? Maybe not. In any case, as I was discovering, explaining it once did not work. It had to be explained on one occasion in one way and then again from a different angle, so that no doubt, at some stage, a combination of the words used, the context, the events leading up to it, their inclination and ability to be receptive and their level of development at that moment would conspire to create understanding. That moment had not been reached. The wider and virtual world also became another aspect to factor in.

'We looked you up on Google,' one of their school friends announced brightly. 'There's lots about you. You've been on TV.'

'Yes, I'm a writer. I've written about Piers, Ian and Lars and how they came to be born.'

My nine-year-old questioner scurried off to play in the undergrowth. Whatever it was he had discovered via the search engine was not volunteered to me. Like my sons, he was on the brink of awareness, but not there yet. There was the method and there were the results. The results were what I had lived with for 10 years; the method was a one-off. Just the results, that really was all that I had been interested in. 10 years before, I knew what the ends would be and the means were simply justified by them. There were my three sons. Fact. It had happened like this. Fact. So now can we move on to more interesting things? No. Every now and then they wanted to know it and then they wanted to know it again. Or perhaps they had not known it properly in the first place. That the pre-10s were receiving rudimentary sex education at school and all sorts of permutations of it from their peers was a complication as 'the facts of life' bore little relation to the facts of their creation. Just as comparative religion was on the curriculum, maybe it should include comparative procreation.

'Did we come out of your penis, Dad?'

'In a way, but that's not how you were born.'

'Then where did we come out? Was it the bottom? Is that where babies come out? The bottom?'

'No. The vagina.'

'Uuugh. That's horrible. Not Tina's v…'

'No, you didn't. You came out of the tummy. It was cut and you came out. One, two, three.'

'But how did you get the seeds?'

I chose to reinterpret the question.

'How did I get the seeds to go into the egg? That's called fertilisation. Dr Smotrich at the lab did this. He took three of the seeds and injected them into three eggs.'

'But there were four, weren't there?'

'Yes, I meant four. But one didn't make it.'

'But that's really sad, Daddy. Why didn't he make it? We could have had another brother.'

'Or a sister, indeed. Well, he or she was microscopic and sometimes such tiny microbes don't survive.'

'But how did they get the seeds out of you, Daddy?'

'Yes, Dad, and what colour were they?'

'Off-white and we're going to have to get a move on.'

Three small 10-year-old-bottoms had wriggled into blue corduroy trousers, striped ties had been tied, hair had been slicked back and down they came to breakfast. The tricky question remained unanswered for a while.

Would I have asked my parents' questions like this? No. Was this respect, fear, embarrassment or did the need for an answer simply not arise? I tried to go back to my nine-and-a-half year-old self, but failed. Perhaps I simply accepted it or was it part of my need to please that I did not want to embarrass them?

Or was it the change from the repressive buttoned-up '50s of my childhood to the liberally tolerant and open 21st century that I had benefited from so much? Already one of the boys had told me, 'I saw a woman sucking a man's penis. It was sooo funny.' He and his brothers burst out laughing. They had all seen fellatio on their laptops. In spite of parental controls, their world contained images that I had not seen until my adulthood. 'Look at what my penis can do,' said one as it waggled up and down in its semi-erect state. Maybe I should see their openness as a compliment, that they feel they can tell me whatever they wish. I never felt this with my parents and so did not trespass into areas that I thought might be contentious.

'You say we're test tube babies, Daddy, so did you wee your seeds into a test tube?'

'You get the seeds out in a different way.'

'Daddy, what's a 'wanker'?'

Maybe Piers already knew how.

'And a 'tosser'?

I suspect he did.

Was it because of the unorthodox nature of their arrival into the world that above all I craved normality for my sons? Their conception and birth had been as unusual and hi-tech as could be. There was my start in life – mother, father, son – and there was theirs – father (who had no legal right to them), two mothers (one who had not met them and one who had signed them away) and immigration into the UK as aliens with no legally established right to remain there. In spite of all this, I saw my family life as normal, my own situation as stable and I was as loving a dad as any. The children had no reason to feel different from any other children and I could only compare their upbringing with my own. It was by discovering on a daily basis how impossible this was that the changes over the last 50 years were rammed home to me and how, little by little, I could recognise that, while my upbringing may well have been normal for the times, I found myself questioning whether many of the precepts on which it was based were desirable.

Right thinking people

As a child, I went to Sunday School. My parents thought it appropriate that I have good, and therefore, right-thinking people as an influence in my life. Christening classes alerted me to the moral certainties of the deeply religious and made me question the very nature of unquestioning acceptance. I found myself looking forward by looking back – looking twice at what I now understood I had simply accepted as a child because it was there and there was no alternative. I had not wished to dis-agree because that was disagreeable and for a sensitive child who wanted to do 'the right thing' there was a fine line between not accepting and not being polite. At every stage, the child who had been me had not accepted, could see no reason for not accepting and so had assumed he was just wrong, but remained polite and took on board whatever had come his way because that was what he felt he had to do.

The grown up me could see the childish me in each of his sons and wanted to enable them to express their opinions, to let them question the orthodoxy of the times, because that, I realised, was what it had been. I had been a product of my times. My upbringing and schooling had not been based on uni-versal truths, but on what was appropriate for people in that social class at that period in time which was so distant that I could view it as the historical period it was. Just as the main purpose of photographs of yourself is that they give you some-thing to laugh at later, I would, had it not been so fundamental and what had defined me as an adult, have found it similarly risible.

The dismissal of the option of Sunday School was easy. Far better to play at home. Out, too, went the idea that a nanny was necessarily a good thing. I had preferred to play by myself. My sons had the bonus of each other to play with and, unlike my parents, I worked from home so I could give them me. It was with school that I had the greatest dilemma. That was an inevitable part of their lives and it was towards the known that I was attracted. Walking to the local infant school where there were kind, nurturing people guided by a knowledgeable bureaucracy, then onto the junior and senior schools just like their father, that was the premise that guided me at the outset. I thought I looked back at my school days with affection, but when I did I knew that that it is how I felt I should see them.

That I did not see them in this way was not my fault. With few exceptions, the teachers in my life had been remote, authoritarian and unforgiving. The ideal would be the truly inspirational teacher who combined knowledge with a passionate feeling for the subject and a love of imparting erudition. I searched my memory for those I had liked, those who had taught the subjects that I came to love, but there was no Mr Chips. Even the fragrant, powdered, silver-haired, grey-suited, pink-chiffon-scarved Miss D, in whose brand new 1958 classroom with slim venetian blinds through which slatted shafts of sunlight picked up floating flecks of chalkdust I felt I had gained the most, came back to me on mature analysis as an uptight spinster holding back her frustrations, remaining aloof, remote, unsmiling and dissatisfied.

It came to me that rarely had I been encouraged to think for myself, been taught how to think, been given the vocabulary to enable me to do so. Comforting though the certainties of school were, they were ultimately constraining. History was the memorising of facts; English was parsing, précising and paraphrasing; Maths was getting the right answers; the Sciences were copying experiments. By and large, the teachers were a collective Mr Gradgrind.

My boys had fantastic and inspirational teachers who ran the range of charisma from quirky to off-the-wall and whose lessons were unhindered by the national curriculum and who I could not imagine in what I saw as an essentially politically correct state sector. That they questioned everything was a far cry from my passive acceptance.

But I found it so hard to come to terms with the idea of privilege. Everyone should have these brilliant teachers, superb surroundings and richness of opportunity. I was tapping 'admission to local authority primary school' into the computer. I paused, reflected, stopped and decided that not deciding was a kind of decision. I would let time go by.

It was only at this point that I came to the realisation that not only was I a product of my times, but so were my parents and their parents, and that my grandparents, whom I had never met, were part of the Victorian culture, members of the repressed working class, all of whom had exerted an extensive influence with the certitude and absolutism of their time. What I had seen as an ideal childhood was merely a safe one. Safe because it had happened and because there were no uncertainties. I could not imagine why I had not seen through this as a child; why it had taken the development of my sons for me to see it for what it was. Through the wrong end of a telescope, it came into focus. I first went to the theatre when I was 16; my sons were at children's productions of Shakespeare's plays in Stratford when they were five. In their experiences and their ability to externalise these, they were way ahead of me. Not only was it impossible for them to follow the same route as their father through their childhood, it would have been mind-numbingly dull for them to do so. The nonsense I rail at that is part of life in the 21st century is just a nuisance. Far more debilitating were the spiritual and intellectual restrictions of the mid-20th century. The message 'The meek shall inherit the earth' was tacitly suffixed with 'if it's all right with you.'

A second visit to my sons' school Harvest Festival helped

me understand the basis for their constant questioning and curiosity. It was far removed from the earnestness of my own school's religiosity.

'My wife and I had a look in our kitchen and found a tin,' said their Head, sweeping an arm towards the abundance of produce, 'And the pre-prep grew a carrot.' He plucked a stalk with a wispy root from a basket. The congregation relaxed. 'And our preacher only arrived in England at two this morning.'

'I hope I don't fall asleep during my own sermon. I'm reminded at Harvest Festival of the Monty Python take on 'All Things Bright and Beautiful': 'All things dull and ugly, All creatures short and squat, All things rude and nasty, The Lord God made the lot'.'

All this would have been heresy in the 1950s, but there it was, part of the smorgasbord of concepts my sons had to choose from in their schooling.

'Let us pray.'

Voices murmured in a low drone. Head bowed, the mum next to me took the opportunity to flick through the pages of her Filofax.

15

Bureaucracy

Rules is rules

S. was a wonderful help. The boys had known him since their nursery days when they were three. He had been enormously popular with the children and the parents and had been the only man there. In his early 40s, he was also the oldest. One day he disappeared. No longer was S.'s scooter outside the nursery. The boys had been used to wishing it goodbye when they left. I asked if he were coming back and, although nothing was directly stated, I was told he had had a breakdown. Shortly afterwards, I had a visit from the Sexual Offences branch of the police. They told me that an anonymous letter had been sent to OFSTED and that they were obliged to follow up on it. I was all ears.

'Various allegations have been made, involving several children, including your sons. We understand he wiped their bottoms after the lavatory. We also understand that he very often went to the lavatory himself. Did you find his behaviour with them inappropriate?'

'Not at all. They need to be checked after the lavatory. And as to his going to the lavatory himself, I can't possibly comment on that. Just let me say that I often have S. help me with my sons and look after them if I have to go out. I have no doubt that he is excellent with them in every respect. I have no idea about any letter or who may have been moved to write it, but I wouldn't be surprised if jealousy lay behind it.'

'Well, we have other parents to see and shall get back to you. In the meantime, of course, you won't employ him with your children.'

I phoned Ian's godfather who runs a security company. A few days later my home was wired for sound and vision. Cameras and mikes were hidden and the data was transferred to a hard disk in a cupboard. I felt dreadful at this subterfuge, but here was a rare thing, a man in early learning, an excellent man whose career and life were being ruined by allegations. I asked him to look after the boys one evening and put them to bed. My heart was absolutely not in my mouth. I was certain that nothing untoward would happen.

The following day, I took the disk to the police station. They looked and phoned me to say that there had been plenty of opportunity, but that S.'s behaviour with them had been impeccable. The enquiry was dropped. No reason was given. S. never worked professionally again. After the Soham murders, any allegations had to remain on file. Although nothing had been found and, indeed, his complete straightforwardness and correctness with children had been proved, he was effectively unemployable. S. had no idea why the enquiry had been discontinued and, as I felt an element of shame about my actions, I did not reveal my part in it for many years. When I did tell him, his gratitude was effusive.

'I never doubted you. I'm just sorry that I had to deceive you to prove your innocence. Not, I'm afraid, that it's made any difference.'

S. was always available. Great for me, but a tragedy for a kind man with a big heart who had so much to give to children.

Hard cases make bad laws. In an age when paedophiles are seen lurking behind every tree and when something, anything, has to be done after an atrocity, this piece of political correctness was an injustice. It was the most vicious instance of many I encountered as a dad. All made me sad. All were more or less nonsensical.

Candid Camera

'You'll have to put that away.'

   'Why?'

   'There's a notice saying you can't take photographs here.'

   Soft-coated scaffolding, plastic covered tunnels, slides, a wall with knobs on and coloured balls had gleamed invitingly. The pedal cars and team races that had been part of the birthday party they had just attended were over, but my boys were not yet ready to leave.

   'Can we go into the play area, Daddy?'

   The signs on the walls of the hut where their party had been should have warned me. In large letters parents were informed that they were permitted to take photographs. No such notice adorned the walls of the climbing wall area. I observed both in retrospect. At the time, all I could see were three happy little boys running and playing as children do. I reached for my tiny digital camera and captured the moment on film.

   'I'm not taking photographs, I'm filming my sons.'

   'Same thing. You'll have to stop.'

   'I'm sorry to sound repetitive, but why? What possible harm can there be filming my boys on your climbing wall? It's not that there's anyone else on it.' I gestured expansively.

   'If I let you use your camera, I'd have to get the written permission of everyone in this room.'

'I'm sorry, but that's rubbish. Actually no one has a right to his own image.'

'I'm following instructions.'

'Look, these are precious moments I'll never get again. These instructions are based on a false premise.'

'Let's put it this way, sir. This is private property and in buying tickets, you've agreed to our terms.'

'What the matter, Daddy?'

'Nothing boys, I am just talking to this gentleman and putting my camera in my pocket as I don't want to have an argument in front of you. Daddy wanted to film you playing. He isn't allowed to.'

'Like in the toy shop?' Ian had a prodigious memory. I had attempted to capture the very first time they went shopping. 'Stop that! You can't film,' I was instructed. The young man had not reckoned on their godmother's intervention. They were there to spend the money she had given them for their fourth birthday a few days before.

'May I see the Manager? I want to ask him what the reason for this is.'

'I am the Manager. We don't allow filming.'

'I want an explanation not a statement of fact. Why is there this policy?'

The young man restated the fact he had just given us.

'Then give me the number of your press office.'

An older man arrived. 'We make the rules and we can bend them. Carry on.'

'Stop filming. You can't say that.' He turned to me, 'I'm senior to him and I say no.'

By that time a small crowd had gathered. The boys had wandered off, far more interested in the toys on offer.

'This is my godsons' first ever shopping trip. It's a special occasion that their father wants to capture.'

Head Office sanctioned this simple request as a favour, but the boys had chosen their gifts and the moment had passed.

Their godmother encountered another jobsworth with us at a theme park on a rainy December day when they were seven.

'They can't go on this ride,' the young operator announced. 'They must be accompanied by an adult. It says so. Here.' He indicated a large notice.

'This kind man has told us that he will go with them.'

'You don't know him.'

This was true. He had recognised us in the queue a few minutes before and, when both of us had expressed a disinclination to have our senses left reeling by the whirling ride we had just seen, had offered to go with the boys.

'Can you tell me where it says 'accompanied by an adult you have known for longer than a few minutes in the queue'?'

I sensed that the queue and the half-full delayed ride were growing restless.

'OK, I'll go.' I felt suddenly noble. The boys started to embark.

'Not him. You can only take two. It says so. Here.'

'Sorry, Piers. I'll take your brothers and come back for you.'

After some minutes during which my stomach went west as I travelled east, I had to change my mind.

'I'm sorry, Piers, I just can't do it again. It was a sort of hell on earth.'

Piers started crying. I was adamant. So was the operator.

Their godmother took the initiative. 'May I speak to the manager, please?'

'She's over there.'

We left the enlarged saucer to hurl its screaming occupants across the Hampshire countryside. I took the boys to see the animals while their godmother entered into discussion with the manager.

'It was 'an over-interpretation of the rules', so it's been sorted.'

'Oh dear. We always seem to get into trouble.'

A diplomatic incident

So many rules and regulations. My track record with these is particularly poor. I see most of them as unnecessary restrictions introduced either because something happened to someone once or there is a fear that something might happen to someone that will bounce back on the organisation and bite them in the wallet. Recollections of my own childhood were dimming with the years and being eclipsed by new experiences, but I seemed to recall that in the '50s life was more predictable. Compared to today, nothing much happened, certainly nothing as ground-breaking as the birth of my sons who would, in the grey and white days of the post-war era, have been branded as bastards and been consigned, with me, to the far reaches of social unacceptablity, but if something could be done without bringing society to its knees, it was allowed. In the noughties, there were hoops to go through. None more so than at the American Embassy.

'Awwh, no. That'll take a *very* long time.' Ian remembered well all his previous dealings with things American – the hours queuing at Immigration in Dallas Airport after his 10-hour marathon tantrum on the flight; the ages at San Diego airport while Daddy tried to check in and reposition the seating arrangements so five year-olds and their father would not be spread in separate seats throughout the cabin – when I broke the news to the children that I needed to renew their passports. Their EU/UK passports, obtained after much regulation-bending, were unusable for anyone born in the US who wanted to travel there.

Now we were invited to 'join the queue' at the American Embassy in Grosvenor Square simply to renew their passports. 'Minors under 18 must be present with both parents' the rules read. It could not simply be done through the post. Leave-of-absence from school secured and armed with birth certificates, old passports and various other bits of written evidence that I thought would come in handy, we had arrived in London an hour early for our ten thirty appointment. Remembering my failed experience trying to pick up a passport awaiting collection at the Los Angeles Federal Building without an appointment, I had booked three appointments – just to be sure of getting one.

'Are we in England or America?' Laro asked after some time in the biting wind looking at the policemen armed with submachine guns patrolling this quiet London street. Standing, doing nothing for hours on end, was something that defined America for them.

'It's the Americans' little piece of England here, so we must be patient.'

Once we were granted entry to the building, the boys made the most of a corner filled with toys that were thoughtfully provided for them to wile away the three hours of their enforced stay. Quite why they had to be present I have no idea as none of the counter clerks gave them a second glance. Nevertheless, the venting of their frustration by dismantling several of the activities and finding they made interesting mallets for bopping brothers on the head ensured that their presence was known, although probably more to the equally frustrated hoards waiting for visas than the staff behind their thick glass screens.

'No. I want my own water. I won't have their germs. No. I won't have those biscuits. I want my own packet. This one's been opened.' Tired, fed up and knowing that they were due for lunch with their godmother, these three active little five year-olds had enough of playing quietly after two hours and squabbled to pass the time. Realising that he had forgotten to have breakfast and that lunch the previous day was his last meal, Daddy's mood was not improved by the initial refusal of the officials to accept their birth certificates.

'Yes, I know there is just one parent named on the birth certificate. It's perfectly legal.'

'In California maybe. They have their own ways of doing things.'

'They're US birth certificates. I'm told they're legal anywhere.'

'Have you got the certificates with the mother's name?' I pulled out the three I had brought, just in case, together with the legal renunciation of the surrogate mother's rights.

'We've never seen anything like these before.'

I bit back the 'Well now you have and will you please let us out of this prison? They are hot, thirsty, bored out of their minds and may have a tantrum any moment. They had passports issued five years ago, so just let us have new ones, please' and replaced it with 'They were acceptable for the passports we're renewing.' The clerk disappeared. 'We will accept them. Do you have the children with you?'

'Yes, they're standing on my feet under your counter window. Do you want me to lift them up?'

But the clerk had disappeared again and the boys remained uninspected – a point not lost on the children.

'Why did we have to come, Daddy?'

'A good point, Piers, one I've pondered myself and one maybe you'd like to discuss with the people here. I'm afraid it's called bureaucratic nonsense. There's plenty of it around and, although sadly you can never become king, you will be eligible to be elected President of America, so perhaps you can put this on your list of things to change.'

But Piers and his brothers had already vanished out of the room and I was thankful that it would be another five years before I had to run this gauntlet again.

16

Male Mum

Cliques and yummy mummies

Sometimes we have had to prove our identities to satisfy bureaucracy. Always we have satisfied requirements. Never has my authority been challenged. Yet in England I would fail the ultimate challenge. Since their birth, I have had no legal rights over my children. It's just that no one has ever asked me if I have.

'Where's their mother?' The lady at Heathrow Immigration stopped us in our tracks.

'Daddy, I've not done my piano practice because we were in Germany. Will Mr L be cross?' Piers' agitation transcended our delay in being allowed to re-enter our country. Lars was flopped against me, ready for bed. Ian just dropped my hand and walked through the gap.

Now there's a question. A multiplicity of answers sprang to mind from 'I'm Mum as well as Dad', through 'Which one?' and 'There isn't one' to 'If I were a woman would you ask me where their father was?'

As delay could be construed as time to think up some story and as we were keen to get home and I didn't feel like making a stand on a moral principal, I left it at 'in America' and we were allowed through.

Immigration officers are not known for engaging in casual conversation with the public, so I assumed it was something she needed to know, although I could not fathom why. I reflected on this incident. It was a Sunday, so they weren't truanting. We were in the correct EU line and our passports were in order showing we all have the same name. The boys were holding my hand and were constantly calling me 'Daddy'. We were travelling on UK passports into the country, so I was not trying to flee the country with them. We also look rather similar. I wondered at the time and continue to wonder if any woman travelling alone with her children would be asked where the father was.

I have been in the situation so long that it's normal for me as a parent to be with my boys without a thought as to gender. A parent is a parent and, as I am accepted as such by my sons, that's what I am. After a while, I sensed that I had become an honorary mum, confirmed when one of them sent me a 'Merry Christmas Girls – forget 'join a gym and eat more celery, this Christmas, it's food and booze all the way' circular e-mail contrasting a haggard, healthy-eating celeb of 51 with the gorgeous, dessert-eating Nigella Lawson of a similar age. The mums I talked to, waiting outside for their children to emerge, just seemed to see me as one of them and exchanged confidences as they would with any of the girls.

'Well, my husband hasn't a clue what it feels like. My mother had a maternity nurse, but as soon as I mentioned it, 'Oh no', he said, 'that's something you need to do yourself. It's part of the bonding thing. Like giving feeds.' So I had to do everything. And did he help? Oh no. He was off playing golf or whatever. He was brought up on a council estate and his mum did everything for him. Had to. No money. That's not where I come from.'

This mum with her new baby was certainly exercised. The

'and that's men for you!' remained unspoken, but was clearly the next step.

'And we were great in bed, but then he came to see me as his little girl and I was just someone else he could control. As soon as I found E, he put a private detective onto him and made his life miserable. Now E's into God and, sexy blonde that I am, I can't compete with Him…'

'He left me. Found someone younger. When I was in Waitrose with J, he said 'Are we shopping for a new daddy?' His birthday's round Christmastime, but I'm having a party now, in June, so we can all feel better.'

Not all the mums were accepted so readily. In my first term, one of the staff had warned me that some parents were 'NQG'. 'NQG?' I had queried. 'Not Quite G…' was whispered back, 'G' being the initial of the school. 'Gosh. I do that abbreviation thing with my boys. You know, the 'U' and 'Non-U' stuff from 1956. The boys know Daddy doesn't have toilets in his house.'

'What does he have?'

'Lavatories.'

I sensed I had lost my audience, but I was on a roll. If she could do 'NQG', I could do 'not quite PLU'.

'And he has dinner in the evening, although U-children and U-dogs can have it in the middle of the day…'

My informant did not appear to have read the book.

'They live in a bubble,' a spurned mum assured me. 'They're just self-congratulatory. They have nothing to do all day and no time for anyone who isn't like them.'

As no one was like me, I assumed that the last comment applied to me, too. At least I may have observed something like it at our first Sports Day. Picnics were serious and to be done in style. On this day, exceptionally, parents were allowed to park in the grounds wherever they wished. My boys had their eight am music lesson at the school, so I arrived early and parked in the shade. I was by no means the first. By the time I returned to the car, it was sandwiched between a picnic table for 10 and a marquee. We had the width of the car for the four of us. If I folded our travel rug in two and if we put our arms round each other, we would just about all fit in the small space left. I turned on the engine, moved slightly forward and looked around for another spot. The mum of a girl in the boys' class noticed my potential change of location and read my mind. Into the boot of her car she disappeared, reappearing with chairs, picnic basket and bits of clothing which she scooped up and, running, deposited at either side of her territory. 'Goodness, you nearly had me next to you! That would never do.' I stayed put. In the absence of its owners, the boys leaned against the table. Obligingly, it slid a few inches along.

Some days later, I walked back to my Scenic with the boys in hand. A mum in a tiny, elderly Micra was hemmed in. Yards of road grime-stained Mercedes was parked, slewed across the front of her car.

'You're so small, you've become invisible,' I said to her. 'I'll move and you can manoeuvre your way out.'

A few yards further on where the school drive met the main road, a new model Jaguar had been abandoned. Its owner exited to embrace another mum. The two lines of cars tried to zip-merge into one stream. Embrace over, the mum wandered off, arms raised, to embrace others. The queue lengthened. The Jaguar remained.

Rights and responsibilities

'Hello, C's mum,' I said at picking-up time.

'Hello Ian's mum,' was the response. A hand immediately went to the mouth. 'Oh… Sorry. I realise what I've just said!'

'The greatest compliment. Thanks,' I replied.

'Mum, dad. You're 'it', I suppose,' said C's mum, composure regained.

'It' on occasion was the right word. 'Dad' could be enunciated in a variety of ways, generally depending on what the articulator was seeking to achieve. As a two-syllable word, 'Da – ad' was cajoling and often followed by 'pl-e-eze'. 'Dad' as a sharp monosyllable was a way of introducing a theme in which the child's problem became in some obscure way the father's, such as 'Dad, we can't be expected to do up laces/eat this awful food/turn off the TV.' With a rising inflection, it was a question. The annoying one for me was 'Dad' in which the voiced plosives were not enunciated and the 'a' resembled a bird-of-prey making its presence known. This was a call for attention which needed to be immediate and was made without regard for whatever else Dad might be doing. If the response was delayed, the reason for the cry was often forgotten. It was generally of no importance and could be disregarded.

Being 'it' could mean being three people at once or at least having three conversations at the same time. This could stretch to four if the other conversations were on subjects tangential to one's own:

'Have you got your General Knowledge sheets for school?'

'What's the old name for New York, Daddy?'

'Where did you say the pencil was invented?'

'Was it Charles I or II who ate ice cream?'

or at odds with one's own:-

'Shoes on while I get the car.'

'Da-ad, can we have a Star Tortoise?'

'Why can't you see the stars in the daytime?'

'How long's 20 minutes?'

I discovered other facts of life – that conversations on subjects utterly unrelated to whatever was going on at that moment could be conducted at times of great pressure, such as when late for school, and that the open door of a car into which a child is entering at such a pressurised time could not be shut until the compli-cated thought being enunciated in its most convoluted form was externalised.

Most of all, being 'it' was being everything so far as support was concerned. There was no one else. There was no one I could ask to do anything unless I paid them. It wasn't that no one cared. They did. But there was no family from whom help could be expected as a matter of course. It was a fact of life that the boys were aware of right from the start.

'Why do you give money to S.?'

'For playing with you while Daddy was working. He loves playing with you, but he doesn't do it for nothing.'

'Did you pay Auntie C?'

'Yes. She was your nanny and it was her job. When you go out with her now, I pay her what it costs her to have you. That's only fair.'

And although I was everything, I was nothing. English Law does not regard me as their father. Mums have all the rights.

While updating my will, I visited my solicitor. 'You know you have no rights to them. No rights at all. You can't even authorise a visit to the doctor. You have no right to have them living with you here.'

I had almost forgotten, or at least had disconnected the knowl-edge from my day-to-day life, leaving it as simply a bizarre fact of little consequence. This had been my situation in 1999 when I had taken legal advice prior to deciding to have children on my own making me the first truly single dad in the UK. 10 years later nothing had changed.

'You don't have the right to make any decisions on their behalf. You've done well by assuming all these rights and no one's ques-tioned them, but in law, you can do nothing.'

It was 10 years earlier, in 2000, that I had first heard these words.

'Under English Law, the parent is the mother and, if she's married, her husband is the father.'

'So if I went ahead with a gestational surrogacy whereby eggs fertilised with my sperm from one woman were implanted into the womb of another, I wouldn't be the father under English Law?'

'Correct.'

'So the woman who gave birth would be the mother, even though she isn't?'

'Correct.'

'And if she were married, her husband would be the father even though he isn't?'

'Correct again.'

'So people unrelated to the baby would be the parents and the man who was the parent wouldn't be?'

'You've got it.'

'Hmmm. The law's an ass.'

For all the boys' lives I have acted on the assumption that the law is nonsense. No one has disagreed with this. Yet although I have obtained nationality for them and they have the right to live in Britain and be British and they have British passports, no one has challenged me so I have set no legal precedents. I have proved by DNA testing that I am their dad. In every practical sense, I am their Dad, but in law, I am not. Under the law, they only have a mother. She has no right of entry to the UK, isn't their mother and would not legally be able to be responsible for them in the US as she has signed away her rights, but it is she, not I, who is their only legal parent. Were I to focus on these idiocies, I could be forgiven for being downhearted, but I don't and won't be. I have dared to be their Dad and shall continue to do so.

'It's great that they've got male teachers now that they're eight,' I chatted to a female relative. 'Such a pity there are so few in early years of learning.'

'I wouldn't want mine taught by a man at that age and,' she glanced at the speedometer, 'if you go one mile an hour over 50, I shall ask you to stop.'

'But the limit's 60. The boys are quite used to my driving. I am an advanced motorist, after all.'

'49. No more.'

'Why,' I asked her husband as she accompanied the boys to the loo, 'is she so protective?'

Although she never connected her concerns to my relationship with my children and, I assume, saw me as an ersatz mum, there was a presumption of male predatoriness that I had become used to, but still found disquieting. She worked as a secretary in child protection and, I discovered, had been word processing documents describing the worst aspects of human nature for 10 years without anyone discussing perspectives with her. I guessed that she was not the only one to become subtly conditioned, although the topic was never raised with me.

17

Religion

Hands together, eyes closed

'Why do I have to say I'm sorry for doing wrong things, Daddy? I have to say this in chapel every Saturday and I just mouth the words. I don't say them out loud and I don't say them because I don't believe them and I don't believe them because I haven't done anything wrong, so why should I say I have? Saying I have done something wrong when I haven't is doing something wrong. I won't say it.'

'Is this when they ask you to repent your sins, Piers?'

'Yes – and repent means saying you're sorry. I'm not sorry...'

'OK, Piers, but it depends on what you mean by doing something wrong, doesn't it? Let's look at what you think. I remember the list you gave me for Santa and I know that you wanted Ian's head for Christmas. Now, you see, that's wrong.'

'But Ian's horrible.'

'That may be, but you harboured some awful thoughts about him, told him you hated him and were generally nasty to him.'

'He was nasty to me.'

'But this is about you, no one else, and the wrong you've done. Some would say that your thoughts were wrong and you should be sorry for them. Others would say that it's only human to have these thoughts and that no one's perfect. This repentance thing is saying that if you aren't as perfect as God, you have to be sorry about it. Seems like a hard task to me and not one that I would bother with, but this is part of religion. It's not my cup of tea, but religion's part of school and you have to go through the motions.'

'Why?'

'Because it just makes life at school easier if you do. Anyway, wouldn't you like to be perfect?'

'I am.'

'You see, even that's wrong. It's the sin of pride. You're boasting and you have to be sorry about it, so go and repent.'

Piers was unimpressed and banged the Staples 'that was easy' button.

'Let's put it this way. We know that M's a ghastly bully and we can't stand him. You have two buttons. One is marked 'M explodes'. The other reads 'M doesn't explode'. Which one do you press?'

"Explodes', of course.'

'OK. Point made and, I hope, taken. End of lecture. But you did ask.'

'If I were God, I wouldn't have invented religion.'

'Well you aren't and he did, or didn't, depending on your faith or lack of it.'

'You don't believe, do you?'

I thought back to my primary school days when religious instruction was 'hands together, eyes closed'. Belief was assumed then. Comparative religion lay in the distant future. There was God and you believed in Him. He was 'Very God', whatever that was and he was 'begotten, not created', whatever that meant. I wasn't sure how important He was, though. The hymn we churned out several times a month went: 'He ONLY is the maker of all things near and far.' So that minimised His efforts, although it did go on to say that He 'paints the evening flower and lights the evening star' both of which are quite big jobs and 'the wind and waves obey Him, by Him the birds are fed' which endowed Him with some authority, but perhaps that really wasn't such as big a thing as 'MUCH more to us His children He gives our daily bread' which put Him on the same level as my parents.

All in all, at that age, I couldn't see what all the fuss was about but, as I was an obedient child and those in authority thought it was worth making an issue of, I was happy to go along with it all. Even now, I give Him a capital H. It was also reassuring to know that my race, colour and country were the best and approved of by Him as 'Over the seas there are little brown children, fathers and mothers and babies dear, they do not know there's a Father in Heaven, no one has told them that Christ is near. Quick let the message go over the water and tell them that Christ is near.' As I already had the message, that must be a Good Thing. Religion was not something I discussed at home, or anywhere. Had I wished to, I am not sure I would have known how to start as my assumption was that the hymns told you, albeit in an impenetrable and turgid way, how to think and that's what everyone thought. My sons' minds were less easily satisfied.

'Not really Piers. I used to, but it was the classes I had to go to before your Christening that put me right off. I used to think that religion was just a matter of thinking that one thing was more likely than another thing. And then I met the true believers, those who didn't just think. They knew. They knew it was the truth. They didn't have any more facts to go on than you or me, but that didn't bother them. Belief becomes fact. And I think that's dangerous. Anyway, you must think what you wish, but that's why you have to repent the sins that you don't think you've committed.'

'So why do you say we have to be nice to you on Mother's Day?' Ian chimed in. 'That's a religious thing and you don't believe in it.'

'Not sure it's as much religious as it is dreamed up by American greetings card manufacturers, but it gives you a chance to be especially nice to Daddy.'

Piers was unconvinced. 'You aren't a mother.'

'I'm the closest you've got. Don't I count as both?'

'No. We've got a mother. Well, she's an ex-mother. Doesn't she love us?'

'She doesn't know you, Piers. If she did, she would. I'm sure of it.'

Lars came over and took my hand, pressing his small body into mine. 'I love you, Daddy. When I'm lonely at school, I go to the computer, put your name into Google, click on 'images' and there you are. And I am lonely at school. I'm not popular. They say I'm a goody-goody and that I'm small and that you're old.'

'I'm sorry, Lars. I can't stop being old, but you'll grow up and be taller. It's sad that some of the children taunt you for liking lessons, though. Just carry on enjoying them. That's their problem.'

'But it's also mine, Daddy.' From this nine year-old was coming the logical voice of sweet reason. 'They push me and pull my clothes. They make fun of my name.' These were observations; factual and with a touch of sorrow, but with an underlying realisation that this is the way the world is and that it cannot be changed. After his brother's experience of having inappropriate behaviour 'dealt with', it was a path he did not want to go down. He did not volunteer the names of the children, nor did I ask. He did not request my intervention. I did not offer it. He and I knew this was something he would have to live with.

'It's every day.'

'Human nature can be really nasty and I'm sorry you've had to come across it. Just let it wash over you without comment, or give them a one-liner. If they say that Daddy's old, just say 'Yeah – and he eats children for breakfast.' Just don't let them see that you're bothered. Kipling had the right idea. You remember, he's the one you used to call 'Rhubarb Kipling'. 'Let all men count with you, but none too much' is what he wrote, so don't let anyone become too important in your life.'

I stopped. That was me to a tee. I had thoroughly taken on Kipling's advice.

'School's lovely and the teachers are great. Why don't they like it, Daddy?'

'Maybe because they're spoiled and have so much they don't appreciate anything.'

'If they're spoiled, it's not their fault.' Piers enjoyed his one-liners. 'You said so.' He waved a finger in my direction. 'You said it's other people who spoil children. You,' his finger found the end of my nose, 'You said children can't spoil themselves.'

'There comes a point, Piers, at which they take on responsibility for who they have become and, Piers, I think the same applies to you, Master Choplogic.'

'But it *is* logical.' Piers was on a roll. 'AND it's your fault I forgot my pen for History.'

'How so?'

'Miss S told me she told you at the parents' evening that I sometimes forget my pen. Yes.' he added in case I might dispute the point, 'And *you*…' Out came the finger again. '*You* didn't tell me. Yes. So *I* forgot to bring it.'

'The consequence being that, if I had told you, you would have brought it but, because I didn't tell you, you decided to forget to bring it? Having given it due consideration, Piers, I would say that's rubbish. You…' My finger came towards his nose. 'You… are responsible for yourself.'

'So I'm telling you you've forgotten our pocket money. I've done extra things, too, like taking the rubbish out. That's another pound.'

Later that day, I realised that I had neglected to lock the door of my en-suite. I sensed the imminent presence of a child.

'Hang on, Ian, Daddy's on the loo. You can't come in.'

The presence remained, hovering, hand on doorknob.

'Ian, if you don't leave, I'll fine you.'

There was a significant pause as factors were weighed up on both sides of the door.

'How much?'

'Five pounds.'

Pressure on the handle relaxed. I felt an increasing absence of a small child on the other side of the door. For once, I sensed I had got it right.

'Dad! Dad! Someone was on the phone for you. I think he was a client. I said you were on the loo and that you'd call him. And then I put the phone down.'

I hadn't.

'Five minutes to bed, boys!'

'Dad! Dad! *Robin Hood* was on the telly. What he did was all wrong. He made more people poor, not less. He made the rich poor. They weren't poor before, were they?'

'Four minutes.'

'If you say it's four minutes to bedtime, you're wrong.' Piers felt confident he was on safe ground. 'You're wrong because it may be four minutes before you say it, but by the time you've said it, it'll be less.'

'Then I'll say bedtime now.'

18

Mothers

Happy tears

Tina had been the heroine of the surrogacy. Pregnant for me with the triplets, she had never once uttered a single word of protest, not a syllable about suffering. So huge was she with this pregnancy that she would never let her face be photographed. When the babies were born and they were in the hospital, she had cared for them as though they had been her own children. Although she loved them dearly, she told me she never saw herself as their mother. From my point-of-view, the relationship had been an ideal one. From hers? She told me it had been so perfect that she never wanted to do it again.

Yet she did. And it had not been easy. And never again could she become a mother.

Although Tina gave birth to my boys, there was nothing of Tina in them. Even their blood group had nothing to do with her.

The boys and I met her on a bright February day just after their fifth birthday at a children's playground in San Diego. We had come to California as part of a BBC documentary and this was to be the moment at which both mothers were to meet for the first time and to meet 'their' children. The boys played happily on the swings with me pushing them high into the brilliant blue sky. Out of the corner of my eye, I saw her approach. 'Boys, let's stop a moment. This is Tina.' I fumbled for the right expression that would describe her, describe her function. 'She is the lady who gave birth to you.'

Tears streamed down her face. She was as uncontrolled as Melissa, whom the boys had met previously, had been restrained. We kissed briefly. She hugged the children who were more interested in the playground activities than in her. I doubt if they had seen adult tears before whether of joy or sorrow and sensed they had no idea how to react, so they did not react at all. Though she had done a fantastic job and I admired her tremendously, now more than before I could not relate to her as the mother of my children. There was simply no connection. The boys resumed their play, barely glancing at the remarkable woman who had given them life. They swung on, unaware of her importance in their lives. I realised that the large young men I had assumed were interlopers into a children's environment were her sons. I spoke to them briefly and reaffirmed the regard I had for their mother, a sentiment they told me they shared.

I hoped they were tears of joy. Tina told me they were. The three tiny dependent babies she had seen were now sturdy and good-looking boys. They spoke to her politely in strange accents. They had seen and been seen. They were nowhere near the age at which they could talk to Tina about how she had given them life and why and what it had been like for her. Maybe this would come. In the meantime, there was nothing more. The family she had created had moved on and moved away. Before the event she had told me she knew that this would happen. I sensed that the satisfaction that she had created something wonderful would be enough and I am sure that it was. 'I feel like a babysitter' she said when she was pregnant. That was a logical viewpoint, but when emotions are involved logic flies out of the window. Her reaction was spontaneous and completely understandable to me. To the boys, it was a puzzle.

'Why was that lady crying?'

'Because she was happy to see you.'

'But she looked sad.'

'She was smiling through her tears. Sometimes when you're happy a little bit of sad gets in, too. She remembered when you were born.'

Later, they reflected on their meeting. They all had vivid memories of it. 'But is she an ex-mother?' said Piers. 'She used to be, but now she isn't? You know, like you had students who aren't students any more, so you call them ex-students or former students. Is she a former mother?'

'She has her own children, so she's still a mother, but for you, she did a job, giving birth to you, and that job's finished. She loved seeing the result and it brought back the experience for her.'

'So she's a retired mother.'

'In a sense. She's retired from the job of looking after you and now she's getting on with her own life.'

'She doesn't look like us.'

'She isn't related to you. Melissa is. She's your mother. Tina carried you. Melissa's eggs, Daddy's seeds, Dr Smotrich's test tube, Tina's tummy. That's how it went.'

So far as the boys were concerned, these were the facts of life. At least they were the facts of their life.

They were two wonderful women in our lives. What they did was of finite duration with long-term ramifications. Tina had carried three babies who were a part of her for many months and with whom she had inevitably connected emotionally. They were taken away and she was left with nothing. Melissa's procedure was brief, but her progeny were out there and they were indubitably part of her. They were positive in their wish for the babies to have uncomplicated lives, content to be as much or as little a part of them as I wished. Whatever maternal feelings they may have had were never expressed to me. I was given no complications to deal with, no self-indulgence of feeling.

Yet factualising the procedure for the boys' understanding removed the warmth of the feelings behind it that had made it all possible. Tina wanted to do something for another person that only she could do. Melissa wanted to use what would otherwise be wasted. Both wanted to give life. Both succeeded brilliantly. The motivation on all sides was deeply human, overwhelmingly personal. The mechanics of the procedure were clinically sterile. How to give sufficient information to provide understanding and introduce the concept that all the people involved did what they did out of love without bringing in notions of self-sacrifice, regret and bereavement was too complex a juxtapositioning of emotions. Best, I thought, to simplify.

Staying in touch

'I've lost my mummy,' Lars wailed. My heart skipped.

'It's here,' Piers replied, pulling out a plastic model of Tutankhamun. 'Under the laptop.' They had just visited Highclere Castle where Ian had announced 'I won't have you stuffed, Daddy.' I paused to make a mental wavelength change. 'Not until you're dead.'

For the first few years, Tina and I exchanged the occasional letter during the year and photographs at Christmas. When the boys were seven I was gently chided for not sending photos often enough. 'We spent a lot of time together, the boys and me. I love them very much' Tina's Christmas letter read. I promised to do better and sent several envelopes over the next few months. I didn't hear from her again. The boys did not enquire about her so her disappearance went without comment. I told them I hadn't heard from her for years and assumed she'd simply moved on.

'That's OK, Dad. She's an ex-mother anyway,' said Piers. 'She never sees us.'

There was no regret in his voice. He was simply stating a fact. The person who had at one time been the most important factor in their lives was now irrelevant.

It was different with Melissa. She made no demands at all, but kept me posted on events in her life. She left her husband and formed a relationship with a man called Anthony who was half Jamaican and half British. The British half of her new family suffered a bereavement in 2011 when the boys were 10. She told me that she was due to come over with Anthony for a funeral. 'Pay us a visit' I said. She did.

In March 2011, she and Anthony came over for the day. It was a Wednesday in term-time. There were lessons in the morning and sports fixtures in the afternoon.

'I'll ask if you can be excused sports so you can see Melissa.'

The boys were unimpressed at this possibility.

'It's a home match. We can't miss it. We're most of the team.'

They were all in the Cs and were quite right. Had they not played, the match would not have happened.

'We'll see her after school.'

I went to the station on my own. Melissa introduced Anthony with an unvoiced 'th'. I presented my apologies as I knew he would be Anthony with a 't'. We laughed. There was no tension. It had been five years since our last meeting, but Melissa was one of those people with whom a relationship could be picked up again as though it had been yesterday. We chatted like old friends about how the children were doing and what we were doing with our lives.

'It should be strange.' Anthony said. 'Our meeting like this with the history you and she have. But it's not. It's…'

'All perfectly normal.' I added. And so it seemed. But here was the mother of my children – our children – and any maternal feelings were completely absent. Was this normal? Should it be normal? It was, at any rate, practical.

'Do you want to talk to them about your role in all this? Do you feel like broaching the concept that you're their mum?'

So casually as if it were a self-evident truth, Melissa said, 'I see it as just a transfer of genetic material. That's what it was.'

That, indeed, was what it had been. But it was not all it had been. Not for her were there to be any diversions down the road of parental emotions. Anthony looked on. I wondered what he thought of the familial situation his new relationship was introducing him to. Whatever he might have thought, when the children came home we all had a chat about Jamaica, which we had visited a few years before, and football and what being at a British prep school was like. He, Melissa and the boys chatted animatedly. Everyone was on sparkling form. The boys related brilliantly to both of them and they did to the boys. Only when I pulled out the camcorder did they become self-conscious.

'This is like being with the TV cameras again,' said Melissa. Keen though I was to preserve the moment, I switched off and the normality of the family visit was resumed.

'I knew I was the ideal person for the job,' Melissa said when the children were out of the room.

She was right. She was absolutely perfect. Her relationship with the children was that of an old friend. She enjoyed their company but, no, they would not stay overnight, thanks. They needed to get back.

'Let's have a cuddle.'

The boys obliged spontaneously and naturally. She was

warm and tactile. They shook hands with Anthony and told him they enjoyed getting to know him. They did. They told me afterwards how much they liked him. We piled into the Scenic and drove to the station.

And then they were gone.

It had all been so easy and so friendly.

Had I been Melissa, I knew I could never have done it.

19

Cooking and Cooties

Cordon bleugh

'How do you do it, with three and on your own?'

At its most basic, life revolved around feeding and keeping clean. I thought I could manage the former, if only to amuse myself. Early on I accepted that whatever I did was likely to be wrong, but I listened to the children and we jogged along. I wished they would enjoy what I cooked. If it was boiled fusilli with a sprinkling of grated cheese and some broccoli, no problem, but I looked to experiment. Generally I needn't have bothered. Yet I carried on with the recipes.

'Piers, what you're busy scraping off is a delicious Marsala wine sauce with cream, pancetta and shallots, lovingly pan-fried. Chicken is like a blank piece of paper to an artist and, on its own, tastes rather similar.'

'I like it when it tastes of nothing, before you ruin it with a sauce.'

'Piers would rather have a piece of A4 than the *Mona Lisa*,' opined Lars who was generally my supporter in matters gastronomic.

This was not always the case, though.

It was Delia at her most aromatic and I had enjoyed shopping for it at Waitrose, foraging for the ingredients, weighing and measuring and getting it just right. Now was the moment for my creation to be unveiled.

'Dinner, boys!'

Familiar grunts came from the TV room where an episode of *Horrible Histories* had just been interrupted in an unwelcome way. The kitchen door did not burst open. No eager faces appeared to view the culinary delight.

'Now!'

Was it my imagination, or had the sound emanating from the TV increased a decibel or two?

'Or I come and turn it off and don't turn it on again before bedtime. There's something lovely on the table.'

Three bodies sloped in. One pair of hands picked up the cat; another pair picked up the newspaper. A third pair was picking his nose.

'Now look what a delight Daddy's prepared for you. He's been shopping today and spent this afternoon getting it all just right.' Who was this distant third person and why was I using it? 'Doesn't this look really yummy?' Sensing dissent with this assumption, I provided an answer. 'I'm looking forward to this.'

'Looks disgusting.' Piers sat unwillingly and poked a fork at the orange-coloured blob of ground garlic, salt flakes, mayonnaise and paprika garnish, mixing its lurid shades with the earthier hues around it. His fork touched his lips. 'And it is disgusting.'

'No, Piers, it's not to your taste. And it won't be if you just eat the sauce on its own. Try it with the risotto. They're meant to complement each other.'

'They don't. I'm not eating it.' Arms were folded tight across the chest.

Tears trickled down Lars's cheeks.

'But Daddy. It's awful. It's got… It's got… 'things' in it.'

'AND it smells.'

It did. The recipe said 'fish soup', so in it went.

'It's an aroma.'

'More like a stink.'

Ian looked at his brothers and weighed up my vain attempts to cajole them.

'Oh, Daddy. It's yummy.' His fork dug deep into the rice and scooped out a chunk of glistening beige viscous mass. 'Really nice, Daddy. Thank you for cooking such a lovely meal.'

'Well, thank you, Ian. The only one who has any taste round here I see. Enjoy it. There, you see, Ian likes it and you know that he's not easily pleased. Tuck in, Ian, there's a good boy.'

Ian mentally closed his nose and attacked the food with conspicuous gusto.

'There, Daddy. I'm eating it. Not like my brothers. I like what you've cooked. Thank you for cooking something nice.'

'OK, you two. You can leave the table. If you don't like it, you don't like it. Your loss. Ian and Daddy will enjoy it together, just by ourselves.'

Ian glowed from within. Daddy all to himself and in his good books, too. His brothers sent packing in disgrace. Life was sweet. Worth stomaching this vile concoction.

Creepy Crawlies

I never imagined that the task of keeping them clean would result in failure.

'Aaaagh! It can't be. I wash their hair every day.'

'Yes, it's head lice. We've spotted them on only one of them, but we suspect the others will have them, too. You have to take them away immediately, treat them and then we'll allow them back tomorrow and…' did I detect a slight relish at my discomfiture in the small pause? 'you will have check your own hair. They're quite mobile. And of course you'll need to wash their bedding and towels. Try conditioner to comb them out. They're tenacious little brutes.'

It was via the chemist that I travelled on my journey to the school to collect them. Fine-tooth comb and bottle of Hedrin in hand, I marched them up to the en-suite. Searching with a fine-tooth comb had been just an expression of meticulous thoroughness for me before this, but now my parenting skills and personal standards were in question and I was a dad possessed.

'Let's get these cooties.'

'What's a cootie, Daddy?'

It was a word I had come across in *To Kill a Mockingbird*. I had in mind the kindly rational, soft-spoken Atticus Finch as a parenting model. Whether it was a boy who poured molasses over his roast beef or the visitors he noticed in his hair, this single dad remained calmly reflective, gently guiding Scout, his daughter, to an acceptance of other people's peculiarities.

'Guests in our house don't have to obey the rules, boys.' I used to tell them. 'They're our rules and we live by them. Other people have different standards and we won't force ours on them.' I waited to let the words have an effect. It was the effect of puzzlement. Seemed to them like an invitation to cause mayhem, so I added, 'But we'll tell them what our rules are and if they break them, we won't invite them again.'

This Atticus Finch had an edge to him.

'These are cooties.' I had poured conditioner over their heads and was stroking them with the comb. Small black objects were dropping in to the basin, crawling out of the vortex of water sucking them to their deaths.

'Life, boys, is a constant battle against cooties. And I'm afraid I didn't notice them this time.'

I should have. I had seen red dots on their pillows that

morning and assumed midges. That my boys could harbour head lice was a devastating realisation that all was not well in my hygienic and sanitised life and no amount of being told that these creatures preferred to eat off a clean plate would convince me otherwise. I had been found wanting, negligent, inattentive. For the first time in decades, I felt shame.

'Fingertips! Kill the cootie eggs' became a mantra before every shower. 'Don't just tickle them, scrub them away or they'll be all over your head!' Piers' hands flew through his hair as a blur. Water and foam spattered through the open shower entrance.

'Do you think they're dead, Daddy?'

'You're the terminator of all cooties. They don't stand a chance. Well done.'

Daily, the boys and I inspected the bed linen for the smallest trace of cootie. The comb, the conditioner and the Hedrin stayed on the shelf as our line of defence against the enemy.

And my respect for Atticus Finch and his creator increased by the day. I have often admired and tried to emulate his steely logic and reason in the face of ignorance and provocation and, when I fail to distance my knee-jerk reactions from the reality of a situation, comfort myself with the knowledge that he never existed and that his creator remained childless.

Paragons of parental virtue, role models of competence, pricked my conscience. 'Didn't I see you in the choir at the Show this morning?' That parent had just organised 20 or more boys at her son's birthday party in the afternoon and was about to depart for the local church where she was to sing that evening. Ian came running up to me with an egg that one of her chickens had hatched. 'He made great friends with one of the hens and I'm sure she laid it specially for him.' Her eyes sparkled and she smiled at Ian who smiled back at her. I had raced to collect them from the party having sought to take advantage of the brief couple of hours of childlessness to put my feet up. Flopping onto the sofa, I found that one of the cats had beaten me to it. Wee oozed from the leather folds and a dampness crept up my back. It had been one of those days.

'Come and have an archaeological dig.' An enthusiastic lecturer had collared the boys at the Show's entrance. 'They might find some Neolithic pottery.'

'I want to go on the big wheel. Look, it's just over there.'

'You said I could look for bird boxes.'

'Why's this Roman penny I've dug up dated 1967? It's got leaves on it so it should be Roman. No, I want to stay longer. I'm looking for shards.'

Through the army obstacle course, over to the cricket training ground, round the roundabout, down the helter-skelter ('giving the grandchildren a day out, eh, mate?') and up all the aisles of stalls we went, six helium balloons attached to the two-tier bird box and yard and a half high sculpture we had acquired en route that weighed me down like a yoke.

'I know it was row seven.'

'Which car park, Dad?'

'That, I don't remember. Come on, boys, you were there. It was sort of, well, grassy.'

'And full of cars. Dad. Why didn't you look? We'll miss the party and it's all because of you. I'm tired and we've walked miles.'

'Dad. I need a poo…'

I realised that the party hostess was smiling at me.

'You can have it for tea.'

She spotted I was elsewhere.

'The egg.'

'Oooh, yes, Daddy. We'll have it for tea. Just change what you've made. No, I'll hold it. You'll only drop it.'

'Quite likely, boys.'

20

The Great Man

Life in black and white

'There's a Great Man coming to the school on Wednesday, Daddy. He's a famous footballer and he's coming to our assembly in Chapel. It's on the World Cup and we're going to blow things. Voodoozekers.'

'Who's the Great Man, Ian?'

'Don't know, Daddy. Can't remember. You've got to come to assembly tomorrow though, and we've got to be in at 07.50 to be on time for Him. You've got to get us to school early.'

'He's Pilter Shitton,' came a voice from the back of the car.

'No. He's Pitton Shilter,' came another.

'He's a goalkeeper,' added the first voice, for clarification. 'He plays for England. And he's 47.'

'My boy told me that Peter Gabriel's coming,' one of the parents told me on the day the Great Man arrived. 'Got quite worked up with excitement. But he's not. He's a goalie from way back. Must be my age.'

'Yes. He's 60, Frannie.' I looked her in the eye. She was another Older Parent. 'Gosh, you're doing well.' Her mouth opened – and closed. Although the pitch was straight ahead, she veered away to approach it via the swimming pool.

All around the field, small children ran clutching squares of paper.

'He's sent an autograph on the computer, so we don't have to ask him. And he's not giving any until 6.30. But it won't be the same, Daddy, will it? I mean, if Pilter Shitton is coming, I've got to get his autograph, haven't I, Daddy?'

Using the squares of paper as aircraft wings, several small girls ran in circles, engine voices droning in an aerial dog fight on the hot sunny afternoon on a lush playing field in the English countryside. Having just been trounced in the World Cup, England wasn't going to lose to Germany in this conflict. The squares of paper flapped like machine guns. A few escaped their owners' clutches and rolled towards a row of four inflatable goals. As the hot afternoon wore on, the number of children declined to a hard core of my three and three friends. One of the friends pulled out a stick of gum and inclined it towards me.

'No. It's not allowed,' I answered his unasked question. Recognising that my headmastorial self was intruding into my parental persona and sensing my sons' disquiet at my authoritarian knee-jerk, I added, 'Is it?' Maybe he had been offering me a piece rather than seeking approval. Either way, the gum was returned to the pocket for consumption later.

Inflatable goals were being promoted by way of a training session for children from the locality. No one was being injured by falling crossbars. I looked at one of the friends. His finger still bore the marks of being squashed in a cupboard door a few weeks before. 'It was everywhere, Dad. Blood and bits and flesh,' Lars has told me at the time. 'I just screamed and ran. One of the teachers fell to the floor.' In fact, the teacher had been running so fast to help that she collided with a pillar, but the original version had more of an edge to it and was preserved in my son's memory. Teachers were going down all over, unable to cope with and simply adding to the carnage.

'So his dreams of being a concert pianist are finished?' I had said to the boy's mum. She was not one to consider litigation. Boys had been being boys. In and out of the cupboard, they had pushed and shoved until the inevitable had happened. In a matter of days, plastic guards were fitted to all cupboard doors.

I had not previously considered the impact of falling cross-bars on the schoolchild population, but it was yet another danger to assess the risk of.

'Gosh boys, what a comfort it is to know that you are just that bit safer on the football field. It's a wonder your Daddy survived the '50s and '60s without cycle helmets or seat belts and the law even let me do wind-in-the-hair scootering on my Lambretta. Ah, the good old days. How dangerous they were. We just never spotted it. For us, it was normal life in which accidents sometimes happened.'

'But, Daddy, did you have colours like we have now in the 1950s?' I thought Lars assumed that life looked like early colour movies from the 1950s, either garishly unreal or faded by time. Not quite. 'Wasn't everything black and white then?'

'Not quite, but it was different from today. I think that's why I don't like throwing food away. It was rationed until I was about seven. I remember taking the book to the shop. We couldn't eat what we wanted.'

From the moment of their birth, I wanted my sons to have a normal childhood and, by that, I assumed that my own childhood was the yardstick of normality, or at least it seemed so at the time. Even before my sons started learning it as a period in history, I realised that my youth of two generations before was simply what life was like then. People knew their place. As the status quo was so little troubled with the ructions of the desire for change, the sheer stability of the time is what in retrospect has endowed it with the quality of a Golden Age. In fact, the social system was rigid; aspirations were modest; conformity was the norm. What did not conform was either illegal, frowned on or viewed with suspicion. And there was shame. Being disapproved of was shameful.

I grew up aware of shame and, in common with everyone else, did my best to avoid it. Being different meant that shame was an omnipresent possibility and it was only after decades of the sheer drudgery of being a carer, of performing repetitively the most intimate tasks for someone else, that I realised life was pretty raw, could be demeaning and depressing and that one grabbed happiness where one could. If this incurred the disapproval of a society whom one never met and whose good opinion had far less impact than one's own miserable condition, what was the problem? It was only when I woke up to the unattractiveness of a post-caring life with no love, no fulfillment that I grabbed the available technology and ran with it. The time was such that the mechanics of what I did to have children would have been seen as shameful, but that time had long passed.

No one, absolutely no one, has been anything other than completely accepting of my family and the way that I achieved it. In a country famed for being deeply conservative and traditional, my new family has been accepted or, at least, I have not been disabused of this assumption. I had wondered what would be the best way to introduce the idea that I had children with no wife for me or mother for them, that I was mother, father, everything. I tried introducing it gradually: the introductory 'I have three sons' would generally be followed by 'How old are they?' I would repeat the same age three times. There would be a gradual realisation and 'Oh, are they... triplets?' would be followed by an assent and the follow up 'How does your wife manage?' This is where it used to be a little tricky. I would try 'I'm on my own now', but that could invite the awkwardness of death or divorce, so I tried 'I haven't got one' but, in the absence of further clues, the presence of a partner was assumed. 'I'm a single parent' would often be accepted at face value and was enough for casual encounters, but if I was likely to meet the questioner again, the disappearance of the mother would be a recurring question mark.

By the time I had lived with my decision to have children for 10 years and there they were for all to see, three growing boys of whom I am hugely proud, I thought of saying, 'I used a surrogate.' 'Used' took some time for me to adjust to. It was slightly less monetary than 'employed', but still had the whiff of 'took advantage of' about it. Then I tried 'surrogacy' as a concept rather than 'surrogate' as a person. That summed it up with a succinctness and correctness that described the position with clarity, albeit also an unfortunate brevity that stripped it of all emotion. 'I used surrogacy.' I tried it as a statement. It was just too clinical. Eventually, 'it was surrogacy' became the phrase I felt comfortable with: a statement of what it was with no subjective overtones, no invitations to be judgmental. I am a dad; they are children; it was surrogacy. I learned to pause then for, although to me it was a plain fact the answer would be 'OK. Right.' and then a move to other topics, to my listeners the unexpectedness of the information needed a few seconds' thought and an evaluation of a social situation for which there is no established etiquette. 'It was surrogacy' spoken in the neutral tones that would be employed for 'it was last Tuesday' and then a pause seemed to take the surprise out of the situation.

The reaction was usually an 'Oh', generally with a full stop at the end, sometimes an exclamation, but never a question mark. Occasionally the 'Was it gestational?' has shown that the other person had a more than passing knowledge of the subject, but usually there is an interest in my describing the procedure in more detail.

An interest. Just that. No scandalised shock horror. A genuine human interest, followed by an expression of pleasure that I could achieve a happy family life in this way after years in the twilight world that a carer inhabits. My assumption, which I hope is not an arrogant one, is that surrogacy has become just another method of IVF in the same way as various other alternative lifestyles have become accepted on the basis that one is free to live one's life as one wishes as long as it does not impinge on others.

As a child, my only brush with anything remotely alternative was when the mother of a primary school classmate became a single parent on the departure of her husband. Instantly, the child became different and, I sensed, to be avoided. There was a sudden ostracization. To be a single parent was not to conform and, even though the child had no choice in the matter, to be the child of a single parent was, by a bizarre extension of the logic, equally removed from social normality. I shudder to imagine how far away my sons, the bastard issue of a single parent, would have been from social acceptability. Any hankering for the old days disappeared with that notion. The mechanics of the process alone would have scandalised polite society and moved us way beyond the pale.

The legal right of society to kill is now generally seen as barbarous, along with the banning of sexual orientations that were considered so aberrational as to be criminal offences back then, and our civilisation has not crumbled. Before my secondary school was converted into flats, I sat in one of the classrooms after all the old boys had left and tried to recreate what it felt like to be 11 in 1958. What came back to me first was the casual violence – the board rubber flying across the room; the ruler over the knuckles; the fist in the back – and the factualisation of the learning process. Rare were the teachers who drew the knowledge out of pupils; who made learning stimulating; who were anything other than petty tyrants. All this I had come to accept as the norm. I had never questioned by what authority the ordinary person was obliged to conform to a normality that was based on subjugation.

I wondered if anyone secretly considered us to be ghastly aberrations while I went about my business as though we were an utterly normal family – which, after 10 years, I was sure we palpably were. If they did think of us in that way, they were too polite or uninterested to tell me.

Watching the goalkeepers practise their skills in the heat of that summer afternoon, it was tempting to muse along these lines. The hours trickled by; the Great Man's autograph had still not been obtained. He finished his coaching, presented signed T-shirts to the trainees and then removed himself to a quiet corner where he gave an interview to a radio programme on his mobile phone. My sons and their friends waited, mindful of the Jaguar and motorcycle outrider that were poised to whisk him off to the next appointment. Then he left. He waved aside their fragments of paper. No time.

'Come off it,' I said. 'These boys have been waiting nearly four hours for your autograph.'

The Great Man stopped, signed and moved on. The crumpled sheets were shoved into pockets. The boarders went to dinner. My boys made for the car.

'Do you know who he was?'

'Not really, Daddy, but we got his autograph, didn't we?'

21

Technology

'We have to be back by seven this evening, Daddy.' Piers was adamant. 'I have a meeting. I could have made it six thirty, but there might be a traffic jam. I could have made it six forty five, but there might be heavy traffic, so I've made it seven. Later and we'd be at supper.'

He paused to let these instructions sink in.

'And I need to spend five pounds of my pocket money to build a new room. Don't worry, it's not an addiction.' He took the words out of my mouth. 'I have to show my people what can be done. What do you think?' He seemed to want to involve me. It was rhetorical. 'One of them said he wanted a hospital room. I thought this was a good idea. Then he said it was for the prisoners.' Piers paused to let me work out for myself why I might agree that this was a bad idea.

'Because of why the prisoners might need a hospital room?'

'Exactly. What was he going to do to the prisoners?'

I couldn't imagine or, rather, I could and it was not pleasant.

'No, I have to think of something else.'

'Who are these people you are in charge of? Do you get to know them?'

'Oh, yes, they may be British, but some are American. It doesn't matter. I'm friends with some of them, but some of them I don't like.'

Through a virtual game, Piers found himself in a position of responsibility. It meant that he had to make moral judgements grounded in his own sense of right and wrong. He was in touch with scores of people. He was well aware that these people might not at all be who they said they were and this knowledge did not bother him a jot. 'I don't give any of my details. I don't ask them to. Some of them want to do wrong things so I throw them out.' He was perfectly happy with a power that was entirely illusory and over people he would never meet and who, for him, had no existence away from the screen. In this game, he had achieved, through earning the approbation of his superiors, an authority that he had criticised others for abnegating and that he was determined to exercise well. It encouraged him to have moral discussions with himself and with others and honed his skills of expression. It was a 10 year-old's equivalent of public speaking and I could see his confidence grow daily.

'It really isn't an addiction. I can stop. I just need to spend my pocket money now to show my people that I have some ideas. I need to present them with something at the meeting.'

The meeting was, for him, a real event with consequences. He had to prepare for it. So swept away was he with his grand plans, I could not touch on the inconsequentiality of it all or that he should maybe learn his Latin vocab. He was developing a sense of leadership that was carrying over into his life at school.

'We've cleaned the shop out of rubbers,' he announced proudly. 'The woman there can't imagine why there is so much demand for them. She says she's going to have to limit them to one each. Maybe she should just buy more.'

He was learning about supply and demand.

'Why rubbers?' I asked.

'Edward and I have created a spy force. Look.' He pulled a stick of rubber out of his pocket. Half an inch emerged from its cardboard sleeve and on this section he had drawn a pair of sunglasses. A wispy piece of paper was stuck on the sleeve. 'That's his antenna.' There were others, each with its own characteristics. 'These are all spies and we have adventures with them.'

'But I thought Edward was one of the cool guys. I didn't know you were friends with him.' The 'cool guys', as Lars told me, were those 10 year-olds who wanted to be seen as interested in going out with girls, were good at sport and gave cheek to teachers. The uncool were nerds and he counted his family among their number.

'He's nice. We get on. We're always talking to each other.'

'Is this spy force your idea, Piers?'

'Yes. Lots of people are doing it now.'

My unassuming and unsporty son was achieving a status with an idea involving a few rubbers and plenty of imagination.

'I said to him I didn't know that he was such friends with Piers,' Edward's mother told me in passing while we were collecting our children. "Oh yes,' he told me, "we've always been friends."

'Well, Edward's often mentioned in dispatches nowadays. Didn't used to be, but now Piers talks about him with affection.'

Our brief interaction ended with agreement to arrange a playday.

'That's OK with you two, is it?' I asked at dinner that night.

'Yes, Edward's a friend,' they chorused.

'He likes my books,' Lars added. 'And the films on our web site.'

Paperproductions.co.uk was the boys' own work. It was an Easysite Live format with which I was unfamiliar and dared not touch for fear I might break it. I need not have worried. They were happy for this site to be their own creation and, while they were initially keen to populate it with the greatest amount of content possible, as their skills grew, they looked more to its quality. When I was their age, I wrote a book. It was called 'The Foolish Girl', the storyline of which is long-forgotten, but the eponymous heroine distinguished herself, when the criminal had been convicted, by asking the judge if she could go down to the cells and make faces at him – a request to which the judge readily acquiesced. My book had a limited circulation. I believe it was part of a library I organised with two or three other children in my road. The books and films my sons created and posted to the web had a potentially worldwide audience.

'We've had hundreds of views, Daddy.'

And they had. A few people had left comments. Some were expressed colourfully and were removed, but most were of the 'like' variety. Lars and Piers would go off with each other or alone and create. The Canon Ixus digitals they had for Christmas were put to good use and the house and garden became the location for many an oeuvre.

Organising fun

I had long given up any idea I may have had that my sons should have a childhood similar to my own. Days out on their bikes exploring the local countryside for wildlife would have resulted in their instant death on the road, and the grey semi-detached 1950s life I accepted as the norm was a far cry from the Kodachrome world that opened up for them. Childhood was a commodity that was widely sold. There were businesses that catered to every hobby and even the merest whim. Industries were built to satisfy their interests and every out-of-school moment of their lives could been filled with developing any skill. That their prep school day started at seven forty-five and continued to six thirty or later meant that I was spared most of the choices that confronted other parents. The choices I had already made, such as a small theatre group and swimming lessons, had to be abandoned. The school day encompassed all their time during the term and none during the half a year of holidays. I arranged holiday activities with various organisations and, by the age of ten, let them decide what they wanted to do and who they wanted to do it with.

Absent from their lives at this point was any connection with the local community. They knew no local children. Playdays were arranged way in advance. They began and ended at appointed hours. I tried the 'can X come and play' spontaneous approach, phoning on spec, that was almost the equivalent of the knocking on doors of my own growing-up, but this never succeeded. I also tried the casual approach, telling the parents of our young visitors that they were welcome to pick them up whenever they wanted. As their nannies expected to operate within certain hours, this didn't work either.

Piers asked me if he could arrange a sleepover.

'I'm friendly with Casper now. Can he have a sleepover at our house? Like tomorrow?'

'Absolutely. It's great that you're making arrangements yourself.'

Casper's mum was of a similar view. 'I'm so pleased he's decided for himself that he wants a sleepover,' she told me. 'Bit surprised, too. He's never said he wanted to be away from us before.'

When the day came, Casper was politeness personified. 'Yes, my dad thought it was a good idea, too. You see, I'm going to Eton, so my dad said I'd better grow up and get used to being away from my parents.'

Generally visitors relaxed as time went by. This one stiffened perceptibly. By nine o'clock, he was sitting on his bed with his overnight bag still in his hand.

'What would happen if I feel homesick in the night?'

'I'd tell you to get on with it.'

He weighed this up and clutched his bag more tightly.

'You could phone my parents if I felt homesick.'

'Let's put it this way, Casper: You think you're going to be homesick, so you probably will be homesick. I really don't want to spend the early hours of the morning discussing with you strategies for coping with homesickness, then waking your parents up with the news that you can't cope with a night away, so shall we just see the future in the instant and call them now?'

Palpably relieved, the small boy called home and asked to be collected. It was a call his parents were expecting.

My boys were less understanding. 'But, Daddy, he can't get homesick in one night.'

'Well, as you've seen, he can. Homesickness is one of those things, if it happens, it happens and I'm pretty sure I knew it was happening. Yes, it's odd that he didn't feel comfortable in our home and I know you did your best to entertain him, but there you are. That's an end to it. I don't want you to remind him of this. It's been a failure for him and he needs to move on from here. Next time may be easier.'

All of us knew there would never be a next time, that this was a humiliation he would have to deal with in his own way. He became one the 'cool guys' and was never mentioned in dispatches again. His dad may also have been a 'cool guy'. Some days later, I had a warm personal letter inviting me to put business in a certain direction. I called the number given. 'The letter felt as if it was from someone I know, but I can't place the name. Do I know you?' It seemed I suddenly did. I did not do business. Our paths did not cross again.

*

A brave new world

'It's a tiny lie.'

'But it's a lie. It's not true, so it's a lie.'

'OK. I won't lie. You can wait until you're 13 then. Have it your own way.'

They needed no persuasion to let me age them a few years. Back went their date of birth from 2001 to 1997. The boys Skyped with a passion.

'But you've spent the whole day at school with Eric, why do you want to Skype him all evening?'

'Because we like it, Daddy.'

And I heard them talking animatedly to girls in the same way as to boys.

'She spends far too much time on Skype. I'll have to be firmer,' said one of the parents whose daughter was on my sons' Skype contacts lists.

'Oh, please don't. It's the only time my boys will talk to girls. It's funny that they ignore them at school, wouldn't give them the time of day, let alone talk to them, but when they're on Skype they have actual conversations. Maybe it's the anonymity, or that they're on home territory, or the little boy plus computer bubble that gives them security or privacy or whatever it is they need to feel they can talk to a girl without having the other boys point their disapproving fingers. But chat they do and I'd love it to continue.'

'What would they have said when you were our age, if you'd showed them a laptop?' they had asked and I had told them that the very earliest computers cost millions and were the size of a room. Way back, it was television, the electronic baby-sitter, that supposedly would give children square eyes and stifle their creativity. That was never my view. I saw it as a remarkably creative medium that opened up a world of possibilities, but television was not a part of life I had come to take for granted as I had not been brought up with it.

'My family didn't own a TV set until I was eight.'

'What did you do?'

My boys imagined that we all looked at the wallpaper in the absence of anything better to focus on. There was one channel and few programmes for children. They were fuzzy and black-and-white. Real life was much more interesting and accessible and television was not an influence on my childhood. Enid Blyton was and it seemed quite normal for me to read her *Five on Kirrin Island Again* aloud to my boys when they were very young. I chose the original 1940s edition which included the line 'George had never seen a television' and went on to describe Anne's reaction to it – 'Anne gasped to see a man's face suddenly appear on the lighted screen of the set. "I can hear him and see him," she whispered to Julian.' They found it hilarious that these characters had not experienced television and quaint when I told them I could well remember the occasion when I was invited to a neighbour's house along with most of the street to watch the Coronation in 1953.

They were indeed digital natives. The television was a distraction, but the computer was a passion, an extension of their creative selves. It was when they were on their computers in the room I used to call the 'small study' that they were at their most co-operative. They had their pecking order based on familiarity with the software or the particular site. Whether they were creating a film or playing a game, they sought and received help from each other with a minimum of bickering. They learned and were entertained. I felt vaguely guilty that the computers were giving them such enriching experiences without my having to do anything but provide them in the first place, but it was a guilt that I found very easy to reconcile myself with.

'Piers!' I shrieked. 'I've become you and I want to be me again. Change me back. Now!'

'I just used your e-mail address to change my Skype password. Use mine and you'll be you again. I'm just playing Habbo with Tom.'

'Tom moved to Qatar, didn't he?'

'Yes.'

'Piers, what you doin?' came a voice from Piers' laptop.

'Hang on. It's Dad.'

'Uh,' said Tom knowingly from the Middle East.

Later, for their 11th birthday, the iPad entered their lives — or, rather, three iPads as they didn't do sharing. Off they went one rainy afternoon to Lars's bedroom. Chuckling came through the closed door. The following day came the bills from iTunes.

'Ian, take a look at these.'

Now was my chance to educate a child into good husbandry, basic financial planning, or to make this an exercise in how-to-set-a-good-example-and-not-to-get-really-cross-although-being-furious-would-be-completely-justified. I cultivated a relaxed yet purposeful tone as I opened a series of emailed bills.

'All these are from yesterday and they are all about Dragonvale. You see? Now here's one for £2.99 and here's another for £4.99 and another for £1.99. Let's see what they come to by rounding them up and taking away the 3p.'

Ian's face was turning puce.

'OK, I'll do it. And then I'll add on this bill and this one and this one and, goodness me, it looks as if it's getting on for £150.'

'I'll pay it. Take all my pocket money. Take the tokens I had for my birthday. Take the Argos coupon. Take the W.H. Smith token. Take them all.'

'Well, let's do the calculation.'

Ian was beyond this. He entered denial briefly, not wanting to see the bills, just needing to know that the steps needed to pay the debt had been taken.

'I want it over. I don't want to owe money.'

'Now if we add up the value of your cash in hand and the value of the tokens and take it away from the value of these bills, you'll see that there's more than £100 left which, at £5.50 a week is likely to take you several months to pay off.'

'I'll do it. Take my money. Just stop.'

'Now, let's think about it. You're all wet and snotty, so let me get you a tissue and we'll see if there's another way to do this.'

By the time I returned, the Dragon game had been deleted.

'Now you still have a huge bill and nothing to show for it. Really, Ian, panicking's not the best way to deal with something serious, is it? It's like when you get angry, say all kinds of hurtful things and then get upset with yourself and end up saying sorry to me. Let's be like Lady Macbeth and 'see the future in the instant'. You know what you're going to do, so don't go through the whole journey to exactly where you know you'll be in a few minutes. How about sending a message to Apple.'

'Like what?'

'Like you didn't know what you were doing.'

'I did. I was getting Dragon food.'

'Let's try this.' I began typing: 'My young son, Ian…'

'I'm not young and why do you have to mention my name? You're horrible.'

'Bear with me, Ian and you'll see where I'm going.' Even Ian, now red-faced and tear-stained, should be able to get the contrast between my composure and his distress. Even if I had to foot the bill, I wanted £150 worth of lesson that he would learn from. I continued typing: 'My young son, Ian, spent time with his brothers on 16 February and a short time on 17 February playing Dragonvale. He tells me he clicked a few times, but not as many as appear on the itemised bills. He may, of course, have been carried away with the excitement of his new iPad. Whatever happened, he was brought down to earth with a bump when I showed him the itemised bills this morning.

I cannot say what happened, only relate what he tells me. If there is no way out of these purchases, I shall pay, of course, and he is aware that his pocket money will be forfeited.

If there is a way of returning what he bought, I know that he will be relieved.'

'Now it's been sent, Ian. Let's see what happens. I've told them, very calmly, what the situation is and left it to them to decide on the way forward. It's always best to be calm. Has Daddy been cross?'

A few hours later, the purchases had been rescinded and the prospect of half a year without pocket money had receded.

'Now can I get some more dragons on Dragonvale, Daddy?'

'Give me strength…'

'Dad, I can't get an internet connection. I can't use my iPad.'

'Look, Piers, it's been a busy morning, let me get on with cooking.'

'But you've got to get the wifi working.'

'It is working. My computer's fine.'

'Mine isn't. I can't download my game. DO something. Phone Apple.'

'You be me. I'm not a computer helpline. You make it all my fault. It's not. If you need to sort something out, go and sort it. That's part of the fun of having an iPad.'

'No, it's not. You got them for us. You have to fix them.'

'Take that line with me and I'll confiscate them. Now go and read the manual!'

'And we don't want Blumenthal or Delia.'

22

Futures

Taming the wild

'Do you think I'll get another chance to see a hedgehog?' At 11, Ian was keen on wildlife. Any sort of wildlife. He lurched from one craze to another.

'It's a squirrel trap.' There it was on his laptop. He had researched it, costed it and knew how many weeks of pocket money it would take to get it, provided there were no fines for misbehaviour in the meantime. It was the focus of his life for that brief moment. Nothing else mattered. He had to have a squirrel trap. A few weeks before, it had been stick insects. Before that, hamsters. I knew that, if I held out for long enough, the phase would be passed through, never to be heard of again. When the first of the nine-day-wonders had been externalised years before, I had succumbed. Anything for a quiet life. The demands were petulant. My denying him gratification was a denial of his educational future, his desire to study small rodents. I would be doing him permanent damage if, in my wrong-headed desire to incline him towards more conventional interests, I did not let him learn in his own way what he was interested in. That a mouse appeared in the plastic non-fatal mousetrap that had been the fixed object of his desires was such a shock that he had no idea what to do with it. He pulled out his camera and let it go. It hopped like a frog through the undergrowth. I told him that I didn't care to see creatures of the wild in traps.

'But you let me have a mouse trap.'

He was unimpressed that a mouse was smaller than a squirrel and astutely observed that size had no bearing on the principle, that an animal was an animal, and that if it was acceptable to trap a mouse, it was just as reasonable to trap a squirrel. The manner of his assertion was not one of sweet reason. Like most of his many sincerely held views, held for the nine days the wonder lasted, it was expressed with vigour and in the unmellifluous tones of the jackdaws nesting in the oak in front of the house. He was sent to his room.

'How about a rat trap? It's not their fault that we've taken over their habitats.'

I was more persuaded by hedgehogs.

'They were called hedge-pigs in Shakespeare's day, Ian. 'Thrice and once the hedge-pig whined.' Pam Ayres wrote a poem about them 'squashed and dead and flat'.' The literary allusions cut no ice with him.

'Have you seen any in the garden?'

'Often. When I've been calling the cats. If it's really quiet, I've heard them snuffling around under the trees.'

'Yes, but have you seen one?'

I had to confess that I had not been sufficiently interested to take a look and had just left them to get on with their hedge-hoggy life. Ian's mind was more inquiring than mine.

'But where did you hear them? I need to know exactly where.'

He had it all planned. He would create a nest for them so that he could he could observe them closely. He needed to know just where to put it. I had gesticulated vaguely in the direction of part of the garden that was uncultivated.

'Sort of around there.'

'Sort of', Ian snorted. 'Sort of!' His scorn was dismissive. 'Not good enough. I need to know where.'

When he was given the precise place, he put down cat food and water and waited until dark. He and I went outside when it was still and flashed a torch where he had placed the delights. Frozen in the glare of the torch was a hedgehog.

'Caught in the act. Well done.'

And then they were individuals

Against my better judgement, as deductions at the rate of £1 for every punch directed at a brother were made most weeks, two weeks pocket money was advanced and a hogitat arrived, to be placed in the exact spot where our nocturnal visitor had been observed.

'They're called 'hoglets', little hedgehogs,' Ian had explained, as he covered the shelter with garden debris for insulation.

'Yes,' said Piers. 'You'll get the chance to see a hedgehog. But I expect you'll miss it.'

The dexterous verbal gymnastics Piers specialised in went right over Ian's head.

'Very clever, Piers.'

'It's what you'd expect from a Scholar', came the immediate response. Piers and Lars had been placed in the Scholarship group for their last two years at prep school. 'Were you a Scholar, Daddy?'

'Heavens no. I went through the state system. It worked fine for me. There weren't any Scholarships to be had. Everything was provided.'

'So why don't we go to a state school?'

'Because I thought the one you started at was too politically correct. You weren't allowed to play football.'

'Great!' Piers was not a sportsman. For him, the outside existed as something you had to walk across to get inside. 'We should have stayed there.'

'Yes,' Lars added. 'I haven't got any friends. Can't we leave?'

'I don't want to leave,' said Ian. 'It's good in the bottom class. You don't have to do anything'.

It was the beginning of the academic year when they were 11. As we drove to their prep school, we saw their contemporaries in their new uniforms walking to school. The local state comprehensive was a brand new building. I had requested an interview and a tour. Well over 1000 children were gainfully employed when we visited. The lessons looked purposeful, the teachers were enthusiastic and the children told us they enjoyed being there. Daddy was told off only once – for chatting to a pupil in the open plan area who was, it turned out, in the middle of an exam.

'You're such an embarrassment, Dad.'

'I believe that's what parents do best.'

The Deputy Head asked my sons what their interests were, what they liked doing at school and gave us a glowing account of his school's achievements.

'But we're full.' .

So that was that. Although we were in the catchment area, we couldn't get in. By the following year, the boundaries had been shifted and we weren't even in the catchment area any longer. That September, 94% of their 'cohort group' were all starting secondary school together while my three were in the 6% who weren't. Even if they started at some point in the future, the friendship groups would already have been formed and mine would, to a greater or lesser extent, be interlopers, newcomers, outsiders. At their Prep School there was the in-crowd and the rest. The in-crowd, according to my sons, com-

prised those who thought themselves cool and were surrounded by similarly cool dudes. Mine were as far removed from cool-
ness as was possible and, they thought, occupied the planetary
equivalent of the darkness of the outermost regions of the
solar system of 11 year-old social acceptability.

'I hold the record,' Piers announced. 'Five years in the
bottom team for football.'

My sanguinity with all his sporting failures was well-under-
stood. For both of us, interest in sport was less than zero.
Success at all his many matches was measured by how often he
avoided any form of contact with the ball. His tactics to achieve
this were almost balletic.

'So I suppose that rules you out of being Head Boy next
year.'

Piers was well aware that prowess in sport was regarded
highly and that his inability and utter lack of interest would
never be forgiven.

They also knew that I had no regard for these titles. This was
common among those parents I knew, although I observed that
the strength of their conviction increased exponentially with
the unlikelihood of their offspring ever to achieve the role.

It had taken me a while to recognise it, but at last it came to
me: Here I was with three children whose abilities and person-
alities were as different as chalk from cheese and whatever
comes between chalk and cheese who squabbled, bickered and
fought and who on the surface had little in common, but who,
I realised, were living, walking, breathing manifestations of
their parent's personality, the characteristics of which had
become altered, even to the point of caricature, but which were
unmistakably mine. There was Piers' sardonic wit mirroring my
own, but with touches of Eeyore; there was his ennui whenever anything sporting came up, which was most days. Ian's head-
strong passions were my own, although without the gloss of

justification I would give them. Lars's aloneness was mine, too, albeit with a loneliness and melancholia that I had long since either accepted and forgotten about, or maybe never felt. And all of this was contained within a unit that needed no one else, that accepted the interaction of others in the knowledge that it was just for a brief moment, but then reverted to self-sufficiency.

'But they should be socialising!' I heard all the TV pundits, all the agony aunts, all the critics tell me.

'Horatio was on the phone to me. He asked if he could come and play, or if you'd come to his house. Shall I accept?'

'No, no!' they choroused. 'He just wants us to do something wrong so he can tease us about it next term. He's horrible.'

The phone call back I had promised was never made. I had no idea what to tell him. 'No, I'm afraid they don't like you and think you don't like them, so they don't want you to come over or for them to visit you' was the obvious reply, but I was too squeamish and feared parental ostracism.

Every day, I was giving out unspoken messages and the children were picking up on them. I could tell that I had become more jaundiced and world-weary since having them, not, I think, because I had them, but because my having had them had brought me into contact with more people than before, mainly younger than me and on the way up. I had been up as far as I wanted to be and was on the way down.

'But you should be meeting people and making friends.'

Easier said than done. They knew no one locally. Like their prep school friends, the boys in their year group were the only people they knew. As a child, I would have walked or cycled to the other houses nearby, knocked on the door and asked 'Can X come out to play?' Going out to play for my sons necessitated a prior arrangement, a lift there and a lift back. Going out into the road, they knew, resulted in a phone call to the police and the dispatch of a squad car. As it was, they were their own play group. They had instant playmates and knew each other well. Very well. They knew all their weak spots. Nothing held them back from saying what they thought at the moment they thought it. Their interplay was robust at best, aggressive at worst.

'When you've seen someone naked, you don't respect them,' Lars told me.

Towards me, they were very frank about subjects I would never have touched on.

'I'm looking forward to puberty so I can have sperm.'

'You're my best friend,' said Lars. 'No one at school likes me.'

'That's true,' said Ian. 'He's always on his own.'

'Piers doesn't treat me like a brother. He goes off with Edgar and doesn't bother about me. Even when Edgar bullies me, he doesn't stop him. That's not what a brother should do.'

Only Piers had a best friend. Edgar was as unconventional and off-beat as he was. That he used to be Lars's best friend was a complication. As I had no idea how my boys responded to people when I was not there, I could only assume that tact was not a trait they were accustomed to displaying and that limited the field of possible friends. I could have paid attention to the tales they told about each other, but that was an overload of information and I knew from experience that their revelations were a mélange of fanciful wishes and hopes with a dash of fact here and there.

'I'm always here' was my answer to all their woes. I could imagine any of them retorting with 'Well, one day you won't be – so what happens then?' But it never came.

Maybe they had more tact than I credited them with.

But it was a fact. I was certainly mortal and my sons had even less of a clue about real life than I had. They, on the other hand, while acknowledging their cluelessness, were sure they had the edge over me – 'You just play on your computer all day, Daddy' – which was quite true, but there was no convincing 11 year-olds that, whereas other daddies went out to an office all day and worked on their computers, this one did just the same from a room whose door was always open and which was just another part of their home.

'Sometimes Daddy's not here. Well, he's here, but he's at work.' I would tell them.

'No he's not. He's just on his computer.'

This, to the pre-teen minds of my sons, was what Daddy did. He played. He didn't go to school, or learn anything. All he did when he wasn't playing computer games was put things in the oven. No wonder he didn't have a clue.

Afterword

1999 was a lifetime ago. Another me. The searching on the web for surrogates; the visit to Beverley Hills; the donation on the sofa in the blue-carpeted room in California. In the off-white goo contained in that small phial I had handed over to the girl at the counter, I had seen my entire future. They had been in there. Everything I love. And here they are now, three 11 year-old boys: challenging, bickering, plotting, inventing, adoring, cuddling, arguing, yelling and all the time simply being. That's enough. They are. They exist.

'And what do people say? What do your friends think?' On the rare occasions I am asked these questions, I have to think hard. Unless people around us think and don't say, the answer is 'nothing'. Nothing untoward, at least. Although I did not see it as an adventure at the time I started on this journey in October 1999, this is what I had imagined I would be doing in eleven years' time – bringing up children on my own in a very similar way to the millions of other parents, couples and singles doing exactly the same thing. It did not occur to me that I would attract any interest at all, let alone opprobrium. The great British public gets on with its own business and lets others get on with theirs. This is a grown-up and tolerant country and, from my experience, one that embraces new ideas with generosity of spirit. I had imagined I would bring up my children in peace and anonymity. During their conception, birth and development, as one challenge was succeeded by another, I was sure that I would be only too happy to let these moments pass from my mind, but I also had the feeling that my children would wish to know from me what it was like. If I did not write it down, the memories would be lost. It was a comfort to confide my thoughts to paper. The audience I imagined would be a small one, just my three sons.

When they were six months old, someone sold the story of my family to the press. To this day I have no idea who it was or what reward was gained from it. It was only from this direction that adverse comments were made. It should be unimaginable that a new parent is harangued, but this is part of the free society that I commend. I continued to record my thoughts and experiences, but had the feeling that my audience might be larger than the one I anticipated. *And Then There Were Three* was published in 2005 and an updated version followed in 2006. The response touched my heart. It seems that I managed to inspire people who had suffered the heartbreak of childlessness and give hope to those who had given up on the chance of happiness. That there are babies alive now who might never have been conceived is a source of great pleasure to me.

What I had not imagined was that there would be another journey and that it would be from one CT scan to the next, with fingers firmly crossed. That I can no longer take existence for granted gives each moment an added piquancy.

Bringing up children can be seen as a chore or a pleasure and any situation can be seen in either light. It also depends on the way it is perceived. Given that it is also inevitable, I prefer to see it as a pleasure and I hope this come across in my writing. Parents take photos. I do, too. To write down events as they occur is rather like taking a photo in words. The conversations of childhood have a dreamlike evanescence which, unless committed to paper at the time, is gone in a few minutes. Proofreading this book has brought back many an experience which would otherwise have vanished, but which now brings a smile or a tear or the realisation that, although I have few of the answers, I have at least some idea of the questions.

My sons must also understand that, when the story broke they, too, came into the public eye. I say to my boys. 'When you're a bit older, you can bet your boots that they'll come, the red-top writers, and what they'll want to see, what they'll hope to see, what they'll try to see are three motherless, loveless, damaged children and what they may not say to your face, but they may well say to their readers, is 'Should these children be here; should they be allowed?' And what'll you say?'

Piers was pragmatic. 'We haven't got a mum.'

'Well you do, Piers, and she's in America.'

'Come off it. We don't. She not a mum. If she was, she's a retired mum now.'

He was right. There is no else who loves them.

'Did you buy us like that person on the internet said?'

In any parenting situation, whether single or partnered, there is an element of presiding over the collision of buckling tectonic plates. In my case, there is the additional pressure of comments a decade or more old, often ill-informed, usually poisonous and, I'm sure, forgotten by their creators, floating around on the internet to be accessed by anyone googling my name or any of my children's names. My boys love to google and what they find, they can throw at me in moments of pique. There can't be many parents who can have 'You bought us!' yelled at them. I know where it comes from and I can forgive it, but it hurts and there's nothing I can do about it.

I am no longer the only single father by surrogacy in the UK. The others have sensibly remained silent. One of them read my book and had a single son. Some years later, he had triplets from stored embryos – and a hospital bill for $2 million. Insurers exclude surrogacy nowadays. He said it was 'the Ian Mucklejohn factor'. Can't imagine why. The journey has only just started and there never has been the possibility of going back, but I have no regrets at all.

Nor, I think, have my three sons.

But we are only 12 years along the way...